Raising Beaut Kids

Recipes for **parents** on when to say **'yes'**

and how to say **'no'**

Mark Le Messurier and Bill Hansberry

Raising Beaut Kids

Recipes for **parents** on when to say '**yes**'

and how to say '**no**'

Cover Design, book layout, illustrations and much more:
Lauren Eldridge-Murray
Editor: Noni Le Messurier
Images: Shutterstock
'Look at Me' photograph on page 24, printed with permission - copyright Lisa Jay, 2009
Tiffany Stewart; author photographs and the photograph of the children on back cover -
www.tifimage.com.au

Published in Australia by Mark Le Messurier and William Hansberry
©2013 Mark Le Messurier and William Hansberry

National Library of Australia cataloguing in publication entry:
Mark Le Messurier and William Hansberry

ISBN: 978 0 9752312 2 7

Fullarton House
Assessment Therapy and Teaching
213 Fullarton Road, Eastwood
South Australia, 5063, Australia

Mark Le Messurier
Phone: +61 08 8332 0698
Website: http://www.marklemessurier.com.au
Email: mark@marklemessurier.com.au

Bill Hansberry
Phone: +614 333 99767
Web: http://www.hansberryec.com.au
Email: bill@hansberryec.com.au

Orders
Orders may be made at Mark Le Messurier's or Bill Hansberry's websites, and through authorised book distributors
in Australia, the United Kingdom and North America
Contact Mark or Bill for more information, for presentations to parents and school staff, and generous bulk
purchase discounts

Printed in Singapore by Craft Print - www.craftprint.com

Dedication

'Raising Beaut Kids' is written for parents who want a connection with their kids that radiates love, leadership, security and the healthiest of attachments. In truth, the book is inspired by you - by the many families we work alongside on a daily basis. You've shared with us countless ideas to cleverly manage the tricky emotions and behaviours of your children, despite it being 'tough going' at times. Your resolve and resourceful initiatives are responsible for our enthusiasm, and for so many of the sparkling ideas contained within. Thank you!

This book is also dedicated to an exceptional and growing group of educators in schools. Those who actively work at keeping young people connected to them, to peers, to learning, to school, to dreams and to healthy futures. You are inspirational. The promotion of schools being truly humane places is a precious and slowly emerging concept in education. We are honored to be your companions in this task.

Heartfelt thanks goes to our wives, Sharon and Christie-Lee and our children - to our own precious families. We realise that every word we have penned for this book over the last two years has been time away from you. Thank you for your understanding, love, and unwavering support. Thank you to Kim and Noni Le Messurier and to Lawson, Millah and Judd Hansberry. It's you who have us continually questioning ourselves about the kind of parents we aspire to be, and whether we are meeting the standards set for ourselves. We could write a hundred parenting books, but you will remain the best proof of the kind of job we are doing. Thanks for holding the mirror up to us.

Finally, thanks to our colleagues at Fullarton House. Your steady, gentle interest buoyed our motivation and perseverance more than you know.

Raising Beaut Kids: Recipes for parents on when to say 'yes' and how to say 'no' celebrates the real heroes in the lives of children and teens - their parents!

About the Authors

Bill Hansberry and Mark Le Messurier are both published authors who work in Adelaide in South Australia, in private practice as teachers, counsellors and mentors to young people. This work naturally extends to providing coaching and an understanding ear and to parents. Raising Beaut Kids contains the essence of what Mark and Bill's clients, as well as their research, shows to be the big challenges of raising kids and young teens today.

Mark Le Messurier
http://www.marklemessurier.com.au
email: mark@marklemessurier.com.au

Bill Hansberry
http://www.hansberryec.com.au
email: bill@hansberryec.com.au.

Foreword

The ingredients of mixing sane parents with positive kids and ending up with a great family is a challenging business.

As a psychologist who has spent of lot of energy helping parents understand and raise tricky kids, I can promise you not all kids respond to the same approaches. You need to have more than one string to your bow.

Most parents have the experience of leaving a heated encounter with one of their kids, dusting themselves off, trembling and feeling like an abject failure. Wise parents reach for resources that will help them to reconsider the ways they are raising challenging children.

Effective parents need to shift their parenting gears from time to time. This is not because what they were doing was necessarily wrong. Those methods just passed their use-by-date. Add to that the experience that what works with eldest kids, may sort of work with middle children, but will a total waste of time with youngest kids and you get a handle on the sheer complexity of this.

As kids grow and develop we need to shift and accommodate so that their families can grow with them.

While it can be tempting to retreat to a tropical resort and send your kids cheery encouraging postcards from time to time, just taking some time out to plan your priority areas with your kids and focus on those makes a major difference.

We all slip into reactive parenting from time to time. Take a deep breath, stop what you're doing and inject, devour and enjoy this book.

In Raising Beaut Kids, Bill and Mark have whipped up a smorgasbord of ideas that will leave you and your family more positive and happier.

Andrew Fuller, Clinical Psychologist and Family Therapist
Resilient Youth Australia
Fellow, Departments of Psychiatry and Learning and Educational Development, University of Melbourne
Scientific Consultant for the ABC series "Whatever: the science of teens"
Ambassador for Mind Matters
Member, National Centre Against Bullying
www.andrewfuller.com.au

Contents:

Raising Beaut Kids

Recipes for **parents** on when to say **'yes'**

and how to say **'no'**

Welcome to *Raising Beaut Kids:* Recipes for parents on when to say 'yes' and how to say 'no', a magazine styled 'parenting cookbook' filled with resourceful, relational recipes to steer parents in the best directions to build better behaviours in children.

Beaut Kids just don't happen! Children begin life by being naturally impulsive, immature and self-motivated. This is because they are young, inexperienced, growing and frantic to belong. In the midst of all this, kids and teens look to parents to show sound judgement, compassionate leadership and the capacity to develop predictable structures, boundaries and routines. Kids need parents who can make the tough calls when required, even when making these tough calls inconveniences parents a little. In short, our kids need parents that know 'when to say yes, how to say no'.

Being a parent – what a test!

In the beginning parenthood seems so natural.

Most of us never dream the extent to which our children will challenge us, and push our intellectual and emotional growth. We don't realise that they trigger a second stage of growth in human beings. They grow us up! It's from being a mum or a dad that we learn so much more about ourselves, and it isn't always pleasant or painless. Our kids provide us with powerful evidence about our temperament, anxieties, frailties, fears, dreams and hopes, lost opportunities and how we deal with these. In reflective moments, some of us begin to see that our children's behaviour, just like our own, has a purpose. It's always trying to tell us something, and we must be smart enough to figure out what it's really saying. We also need to be honest enough to acknowledge how their behaviour makes us 'feel'. Only then, can we look at whether our response is actually refining their behaviour and improving our relationship with them. Yes, Raising Beaut Kids has as much to do with our relationship with them as it has to do with shaping their behaviour – the two go hand in hand.

The all-important 'relationship' balance

As parents, the best way to keep our 'relationship' with the kids in check is by continually reviewing what our interactions with them look and sound like, especially when things get tough. Life with kids is always easier when we retain a respectful and friendly air - the notion of keeping the big picture in focus, not sweating over the small stuff and being mindful of our moods and emotional tone. Life also improves when we deliberately construct opportunities to connect; times to talk, listen, share, laugh and play. On the flip side, just watch the kids bite back, withdraw or become reactive when we get too snippy at them for too long! Parents who know 'when to say yes and how to say no' are able to make expectations clear, or, when necessary, let the kids matter-of-factly experience the consequences of poor choices, whether they just happen or are intelligently imposed.

It's from being a mum or a dad that we learn so much more about ourselves, and it isn't always pleasant or painless.

Learn your style by parenting in windows

A helpful way to think about how our kids experience our parenting style - how we lead and use authority - is to use the Social Control Window (McCold and Wachtell, adapted from Glaser, 1969). It offers two broad styles of 'parenting' or 'being in authority'.

Style one:
Firmness, how 'strict' our kids see us as being
When we are high on firmness we set tight behavioural boundaries so our kids experience the limits fast. When they don't meet our expectations we call them on it to keep them accountable. "What consequences should be dished out, and how tough should they be?" are key questions asked by parents who work at this high end of firmness.

Style two:
Fairness, how 'nice' our kids see us as being
When we are high on fairness we're absorbed by encouraging approaches; flexibility, nurturance, tolerance, and leniency. We try to be highly sensitive to the needs of the kids. We value good relationships with our children and always try to understand what might be driving their behaviour. Sometimes our quest to be flexible and fair can trigger us to make too many excuses for them.

As we merge these two general 'parenting styles' into the Social Control Window you can see that four possible leadership styles are generated.

The Social Control Window

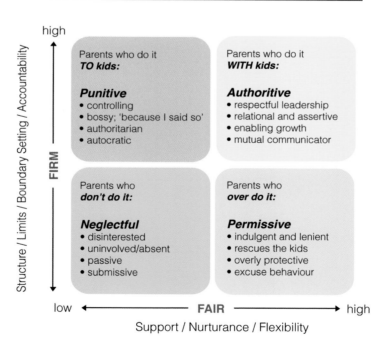

Adapted from Wachtel & McCold (2001)

Remember, your style is the one that your kids experience, it's not the window you 'think' you work from, or 'wish' you could work from. Hey, don't despair, because in truth, all of us spend time in each of the four windows. The length and intensity of our visits are ruled by our emotional states; moods, motivations, engagement, levels of stress, how fresh we feel and other life forces. Most of us are able to identify a window we tend to live in, a window we default to when the going gets tough, and a window that would be healthier to spend a lot more time in.

So, let's begin the unveiling! But, try not to interpret each window as a 'good' or 'bad' parenting style. This exercise isn't about rating one window against another; after all there are fifty shades of grey on the fairness and firmness continuums. We're far more concerned with understanding the range of helpful strategies we have to choose from when managing our kids.

Punitive parenting

regularly hear yourself saying, "whose fault was that?" "who's to blame?" or "what's the right punishment?" You quickly take on the role of detective, judge and executioner. Your motive is always to rebalance the scales of justice and bring the kids back in line so they learn their lesson quick smart. Rarely does the chosen consequence take into account how others may have been affected by their actions, and how those in trouble might make amends with others for their misdeed. The fact is that one of your rules has been broken and to maintain order, someone has to feel the sting. Without this, the family could slip into anarchy.

Sadly, those who manage their children exclusively from this window draw from a very narrow tool box and rely on how loud they can yell, how intimidating they can be or how much they can take away from their children. These tools make some kids nervy, and motivate others to be confrontational, oppositional and highly reactive. And, as kids grow into young teens, there is usually a point where they begin to seek fabulous entertainment from a mum or dad's predictable and emotionally charged reactions - the punitive buttons are so much fun to push and parents become sport for kids. Despite your supposed power and your longwinded

You're in authority! You've got to be the boss, got to have the final say and know how to deliver the sting in your tail so it hurts. You are strict, demanding and controlling, but offer the kids little emotional support and empathy. The famous Barbara Coloroso, in "Kids Are Worth It!" described you as a 'brick-wall parent'. Got the idea? Sure, you love the kids deeply, but believe that if they're to turn out well you have to be demanding of high standards. As a 'Tiger Mum' or 'Tiger Dad' you insist on the '3R's': right, respect and responsibility. You keep the lid on unruly behaviour by closely supervising their thoughts, controlling their friendships, school activities and pushing them in directions that you believe best. You believe that you do this for their benefit because without your relentless input they could very well lose their way in life. That 'slippery slope' is never far away!

You've learnt to trot out emotionally confronting phrases and threats to the kids when things aren't going so well; "you must," "you will," "you won't," "I want," "I want it," "I want it now," "how many times do I have to ask," "if you make me ask one more time you'll

lose your...", "don't make me come over there" and "don't you dare!" You never admit your mistakes openly and don't apologise to the kids when you make mistakes that affect them. In your eyes these are displays of weakness that the kids may take advantage of.

Sometimes you sense disapproval from friends and relations about the

> *...the punitive buttons are so much fun to push and parents become sport for kids.*

uncompromising way you manage the kids, but you justify what you do because they don't know your kids like you do. Nor do they have the 'special insights' into your children that you do.

When things go wrong, just as they do for all of us, your attention is on what went wrong, finding the culprit and finding a way to let them feel your disapproval, scorn or revenge. You

rants, they've sussed you out and work around you when they have to, or want to. In the end, you have taught your kids a highly controlling and confrontational way to deal with others which will affect their social relationships, and may very well come back to bite you the day they grow to a size that makes them your physical match.

Neglectful parenting

You offer little support and guidance to your kids. You are unavailable to give them the love and attention all children need to attach to their parents. You're not strict, nor are you emotionally responsive - actually, nothing much is happening between you and the kids. In your own way you love them, but they just take more time, energy and effort than you have, well, at least at the moment.

Truth is, there may be very good reasons for this. You may be struggling with poor health, relationship issues, depression, alcohol abuse, substance addictions or perhaps you're overwhelmed by impossible financial pressures. And, if you do have plenty of money, rather than giving the kids your time and affection, you shower them with the latest toys and gadgets instead. The supply of material possessions has become your interface and you spoil them, hoping the things you buy will fill the void that your emotional absence has created. Even worse, perhaps you have a wildly mistaken belief that dragging children up without loving connectedness will toughen them up, readying them to

...we've all been here from time to time... Remember distancing yourself from them, choosing not to respond, ignoring behaviours that really shouldn't have been ignored.

deal with the hardships that await them in the future? Or, even grimmer, you may be contending with a genuinely disconnected personality where it is difficult for you to reach out and consistently show affection. In the final analysis, regardless of what motivates your neglect, your expectations and contact with the kids become small because this lessens the likelihood of discussions and disputes with them.

We know what you're thinking. You've just taken the moral high ground and believe there's no way you could possibly fit into the neglectful window. Not so - we've all been here from time to time. Think back; what about that Sunday afternoon when the kids were driving you mad? Remember

feeling annoyed, fed-up and over them. Remember, distancing yourself from them, choosing not to respond, ignoring behaviours that really shouldn't have been ignored. For a mini-moment you placed yourself in the neglectful window. There is no judgement here. Our point is that we need to acknowledge it happens, and we need to be aware when it's happening to determine whether it is appropriate in that moment.

Permissive parenting

A permissive style is in direct contrast to parents who rely on heavy handed punitive tactics. As a permissive or 'jellyfish parent' you offer the kids loads of care and encouragement - you love them to bits! You're not strict, rarely consistent and don't follow through when it comes to following expectations and applying consequences. You don't have the capacity to set up structures, rules, routines and expectations in their lives. You tend to serve them in an easy-going, lenient and 'friendshippy' style. You've replaced 'relationship' with 'friendship'. You love being their friend and quietly admit that your kids are the 'best friends' you always dreamt of. Given the complication, it's easy to see why you excuse and downplay your children's obnoxious and tricky behaviours. You are their most fervent supporter and take massive offence to those who challenge your kids at school, in the local playground or at the supermarket, even when they need to be challenged about their anti-social behaviour. You are their greatest protector and excuser. You are the classic 'helicopter' or 'cottonwool' parent. Others see this but you don't.

You may make light of your children's less-than social behaviour by documenting your highly embarrassing outings with your kids on facebook. You've given up on the dream that your children will ever be well behaved in waiting rooms or supermarkets. You've decided your children are especially 'spirited' and that there are two types of kids: the calm and compliant ones that the lucky parents get, and kids like yours. You think it's just luck of the draw! Make no mistake, you're in deep denial!

The illusion created by your denial means that you are blind to your permissiveness. You have little or no self-awareness and because of this, you take in what others say through your permissive parent lens. Yes, you're always inclined to reinterpret sensible parenting advice and use it permissively. To illustrate this dominant permissive trait, a couple we worked with during our *'What's the Buzz?'* social skills program (w w w . w h a t s t h e b u z z . n e t . a u) were given advice to use the 90%/10% rule with their daughter. This sensible 'rule of thumb' promotes the idea that parents try to shift what they focus on by tactically ignoring 90% of their child's slightly irritating, attention seeking behaviour, and focus on the 10% of behaviours, misbehaviours, that really matter. This permissive couple's interpretation was to completely ignore their daughter's disruptive and inconsiderate behaviour, and disregard the use of consequences or the notion of accountability. The 'permissive parent lens' has a lot to answer for!

Despite your blinkers, you do have one reoccurring source of frustration. It's when the kids end up being disrespectful to get their way. Your first reaction to their rude behaviour is to apologise to them for not delivering what they want, even when the demand is unreasonable.

You fear saying 'no' to them because you worry about the threat of reprisal - they know that you'll back down.

"You've replaced 'relationship' with 'friendship'... you excuse and downplay your children's obnoxious and tricky behaviours... you take massive offence to those who challenge your kids at school, in the local playground or at the supermarket, even when they need to be challenged about their anti-social behaviour. You are the classic 'helicopter' or 'cottonwool' parent.

What you haven't grasped is the reason why they push you to breaking point. All kids push to work out how far you'll let them go in order to find where the limits are. Your poor kids are literally 'feeling their way in the dark' for a wall that never stays still and leaves them feeling out of control. A child's search and discovery of boundaries is vital to help them to feel secure; it's all a part of belonging, attaching, fitting in and feeling safe. Your child's behaviour is actually a plea – "please show me where the boundaries are so I can stop!" You just haven't worked this out yet.

Suddenly, when you are pushed too far you SNAP! As soon as you snap, you become a raging 'brick-wall' parent. Your talk becomes nasty and your response is hard hitting, often vengeful. When five minutes in time out would have done (which you were typically unwilling to enforce), you find yourself removing their iPod for a month, telling them how much you sacrifice for them to make sure they have nice things and how you don't deserve to be treated this way. It's your desperate attempt to restore what you see as a rightful balance to the relationship. Then, when

you hand the hard hitting punishments out, the kids become resentful, surly and angry because you were too severe.

A few hours later, or the next day, once your emotion has settled and your guilt has caught up, you know that you acted too quickly and spoke too harshly. So, to make things 'right' you jump back to being lax, lenient and laissez-faire. You return to your reluctance to use sensible, well placed consequences. It's what you know. It's become a well-honed habit. From time to time you'll deliver an exaggerated apology for your overblown actions, but it's all about sucking back up to the kids.

You wouldn't be surprised to learn that kids exposed to this swinging situation often end up confused. The influence of you jumping from one window to another on children is muddling. They lose their 'sense of self'; their esteem, and what they are really capable of. Over time these kids become highly vulnerable as they are often attracted to marginalised groups, such as gangs, cults and bullies who have a worrying power over them because they yearn for a sense of structure, belonging and consistency.

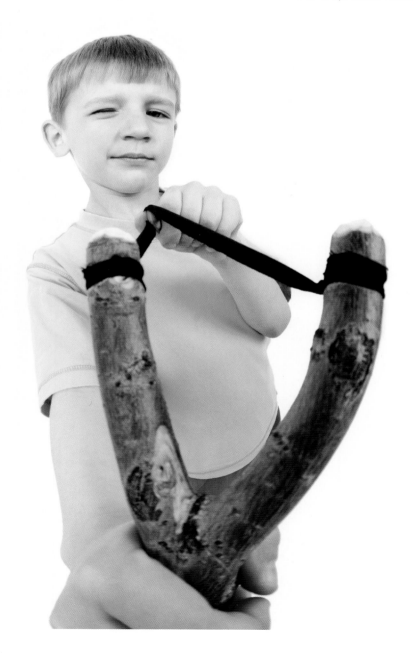

Authoritative parenting

The research supports authoritative parenting as most effective for Raising Beaut Kids. Working in this window you offer the kids high levels of understanding, encouragement, nurturance and love. Likewise, you make expectations clear by cooperatively developing suitable limits, structures and boundaries.

You read your kids well because you're actively involved in their lives - you choose to know them. You sit together as a family for dinner, you gently encourage conversation, you know what they do and how they feel about things, you value honest communication and expect helpful behaviours from your kids. You know they won't always get it right, and when they make mistakes, you'll let them know and be prepared to walk alongside them offering succinct guidance as it's needed. You understand the balance between encouraging their independence, smothering them, offering too much advice and being too critical.

Mostly, you try to create an air of warmth and respect. However, when a problem does arise you're able to deal with it so the kids are left feeling relatively comfortable about the re-direction. They won't thank you for it, but you can live with being out of their favour for a while because you are a secure grown-up. In fact, the act of re-direction often strengthens connections between the kids and you. And, when it is you who makes a mistake, you're able to apologise

to your kids sincerely. You're rarely challenged by the everyday problems and conflicts that crop up because you understand they are inevitable - that's life! Instead, you try to seize on these setbacks and hiccups as valuable learning opportunities for the kids.

You recognise that respect has less to do with you being 'the mother' or 'the father', and much more to do with how you get along with each other. You talk regularly with them, whether it is informally or at organised family meetings. As you talk you deliberately use words and phrases such as "us" "we" and "our family", encouraging that family unity is highly prized. You constantly follow up, revisit and adapt rules and expectations in an emotionally steady manner, giving everyone a say. Your talk is centred on ways to find improvement, repair and strengthen relationships and make things right again when they go wrong.

Well, there you have it; that's the Social Control Window. Doesn't it clarify how we parent, how we see ourselves and how others see us?

- What did you learn about your parenting style?
- Do you know which window your instinctive attitudes influence you to 'live in'?
- Does the management style you rely on at home mirror how you manage at work, or in public?
- Have you worked out, when the pressure is really on, which window do you snap into?
- Is your parenting style working for you?
- Is it likely to work for you in the future as the kids mature?

Your homework

The next time you're faced with one of those 'classically tricky moments' with the kids, ask yourself;

Which window do I 'feel' like reacting from?
Should I move to another window?
If I need to move, how can I gather the energy and poise to do this?
Which window is most likely to result in a constructive solution, and has a good chance of keeping our relationship intact?

In the end, parents who Raise *Beaut Kids* know how to apply 'when to say *yes*, how to say *no*'.

My Notes:

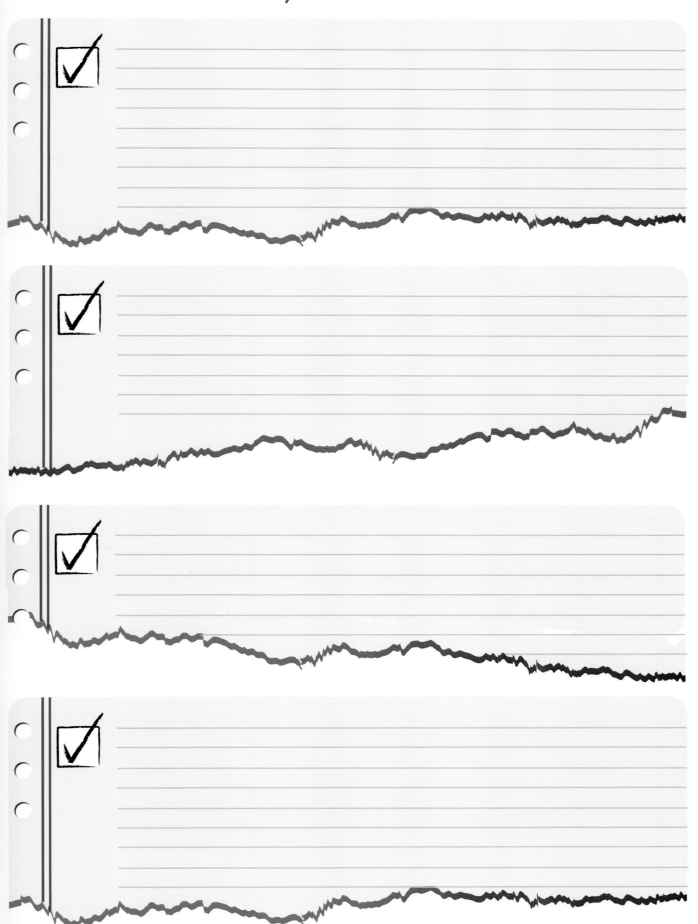

Chapter 1:
Rules

Ingredients:

- **A frazzled parent seeing their child's behaviour as; inconsiderate, disobedient or dangerous**
- **A moment of tension that prompts mum or dad to regain control**
- **A parent feeling as though they must take the upper hand by making up new rules 'on the spot'**
- **Children switching off their listening and 'good sense' because their dignity is being threatened**
- **A history of encounters that cause bad feelings and deliver poor outcomes**

Recipe rescue:

building rules that work

The scenario...

Act 1, "It wasn't us, mum"

Mum (Exasperated, red faced and in lecture mode)
"Oh, come on… I can't believe it. This makes my blood boil! What were you thinking? You weren't thinking at all, were you? Were you? Look at my beanbag! You've wrecked it and look at the mess! Oh yes, you'll clean up every last bit by hand – not with my vacuum cleaner. How many times have I told you not to hit each other with the beanbag? How many times have I caught you doing this before? I've been over and over and over and over it with you. It's as if you don't hear me, don't respect our things and don't care. I asked all of you to be good while I was away for those few minutes. I may as well have saved my breath! You don't listen – you never do! Abby, what were you doing when this happened? You're the oldest. You know I rely on you. I'm so disappointed. You're grounded!"

Abby (Resigned to copping it because she's the oldest)
"Mum, you can't ground me for this. It wasn't my fault. I was doing my homework in my bedroom. I can't watch all of them all the time. I've got a life you know!"

Caleb (The youngest)
"I didn't do it, mum"

Alex, Ross and Dottie (In unison)
"It wasn't us, mum"

Mum
"Then who's to blame? Who wants to own up!"
(Mum waits for an answer. There's silence. The kids gaze at the floor. No answer is forthcoming)
"Just as I thought! You all know better than this. You know this is not on! From now on the 'new rule' is that none of you will come into the lounge room ever again. Not for anything or for any reason at all. It is strictly and totally out of bounds."
(An exasperated mum walks away leaving the kids to clean up)

Doesn't it make you think about how 'new rules' actually spring to life in our homes?

In this instance, mum made a 'new rule' up on the run to appease her disappointment and the annoying behaviours she was dealing with. If we're honest with one another, it's the high stress moments that have the dimension to wreck our best intentions. In an emotionally charged state, as we desperately try to demonstrate leadership, or reassert our authority, the establishment of a 'new rule' is usually accompanied by at least a little yelling, lecturing, preaching, martyrdom and complaining at our kids. In our heated state we virtually go head to head with the kids as if we're in a boxing ring with them. In the sanity of this quiet moment our well-developed adult logic tells us that this approach is completely fruitless.

Did you know that the listening capacity of kids only stretches to receiving several words in moments of high tension? We know that the window for them to listen and care is very small and even smaller when they feel threatened. There is no reaching them once their shutters come down! What our kids absorb is mum or dad nagging or over-reacting again. The rapid rise in our emotion always deflects from the heart of the problem and how-to find a meaningful solution.

Questions and answers

Q: How many of us have made up a 'new rule' for the kids in high stress moments?
A: Most of us.

Q: So, why do we do it?
A: It's spawned by our frustration and a misguided bid to take back control in that moment.

Q: Does the 'new rule' then stand the test of time?
A: No, because usually it's too strict to police, has no support from anyone and the kids actually enjoy getting around it because they feel thwarted! The hastily made 'new rule' rarely gives rise to any constructive changes.

Isn't it odd that we know this, but can't seem to get it right in the moment when it really counts? Yes, great management skills are deceptive. There's so much more to it than knowing what to do. There's a considerable divide between those who say they have the answers compared to those who have them, and can actually put the skills into place when under pressure. When under pressure, so many of us admit to falling headlong into the obvious pitfalls.

Recipe rescue:

building rules that work

In this Recipe rescue let's move beyond the limited idea of making 'new rules' up on the run. Instead, let's become strategic, educational and promote four key foundation ideas necessary for every family;

1. A family mission statement
This captures the positive potentials you see in your family, and emotional capacity you want to develop. It is a unique personal description of your family. Sounds clichéd, right? Suspend your judgement for a moment!

2. Family meetings
These bring your family mission statement to life. They provide a forum for each family member to raise questions, discuss problems, celebrate successes and forge new directions in the company of one another.

3. Family rules (or values)
These are built at the family meeting and are based on the family mission statement. Clarifying rules delivers a sense of structure, expectation and belonging. It makes it clear how-to treat and live with one another.

4. A family motto
This can be the icing on the cake. In essence, it sums up how a family lives and works together. For example, "Hansberry's stick together" and "Le Messurier's never give up".

A family Mission Statement

Yes, we agree it does sounds a little USA, rah, rah, rah and corporate, but the benefits can't be dismissed *(Covey, 2004)*. Its purpose is to help everyone move in the same optimistic direction; see it as a road map! Get the family together and ask the kids; "If a visitor came into our house and watched us all working together really well, how they would describe us and what was happening?"

Break this question down into specific questions;

- What would be happening between each of us?
- How would we be treating each other?
- How would each of us be feeling?
- How would we be talking to one another?
- What would we be doing for each other?
- What would they see as we sorted out a disagreement?
- What qualities would be admired?

The answers to these questions are the first step towards creating a 'shared idea' of what your family looks like when it's

working really well. As the suggestions begin, and there will be plenty, start to record adjectives and phrases that everyone agrees on. Possible ideas might include; showing respect, love, honesty, care, fairness, giving privacy, helping, being kind of one another, enjoying spending time together, celebrating each other's successes and creating a relaxed home where friends are welcome. During the discussion, gently and wisely, insert several aspects that you value;

- the way money is shared, saved and spent
- how the computer is used
- the significance of education and future
- the amount of family time spent together
- how the family contributes to the wider community
- the importance of sport and other activities outside of the home
- individual responsibilities each family member has towards maintaining the household

Now you have a broad brush stroke of what your family thinks matters most.

What's next?

1. For those of you with older children the next step is to place their positive suggestions, phrases and adjectives into brief family statements. Be clever here - less is best - so aim at no more than five statements that capture your mission. Here are five statements we've drawn out from the 'shared ideas';

Edit your statements until everyone agrees with the words, but especially with the sentiment. Keep words to a bare minimum.

2. For those of you with younger children pull out six, seven or eight key words from the 'shared ideas' you generated together. Place these (you might like to print them on the computer to make them look consistent and 'artistic') on to a large sheet of poster paper - don't glue them yet! Next, ask each family member (adults included) to choose one of the printed words that is special to them and role-play how that quality would look in real life. Once they have perfected it take a photograph of them doing it. Presto, you now you have that special family quality captured forever! Print the photo and place it on the poster next to the word. Get the arrangement right and glue. Don't forget to leave space at the top of the poster to add your personalised heading... 'Our Family Mission Statement' or 'What our family is about' or 'The Jones' believe in...' and so on.

Finally, purchase a cheap frame and frame your family's mission statement. Hang it where everyone can see it, including visitors to your home! This is an important step because a public commitment tends to make each of us work a little harder! Once that mission statement goes up on the wall, it's up to the grownups to demonstrate a commitment by modelling the behaviours on it. So, next time you start to unravel and your temper begins to take off, just wait until you catch a glimpse of the Family Mission statement from the corner of your eye! Oh, yes, it will pull you up. But there's worse - wait until you're in full flight and one of your children innocently reminds you of the family mission. It will happen.

Family meetings

We've got to jump in fast here. You see, family meetings were used by Carol and Mike Brady, the fictional parents of the 'Brady Bunch' (1969-1974). Sadly, their slick, smarmy sitcom approach did irreparable damage to this dynamic communication tool. So before reading on, let's cast aside any prejudices stemming from the Brady Bunch! Family meetings, breathe life into the mission statement. Without this vehicle - and, it is a vehicle that can be constructed to suit your personality and your family's style - the mission statement is likely to fade away. Weekly, fortnightly or monthly family meetings provide a forum for each person to raise questions, discuss problems, share ideas, celebrate successes and make rules in the company of one another.

A stepped approach to family meetings

First, set up a schedule for family meetings. Too frequent and people will tire of them, too infrequent and you run the risk of only calling meeting to discuss problems.

Now is the time to fine-tune your thinking - family meetings need to be enjoyable - not filled with conflict, disagreements and more demands.

Set aside time after dinner (or even over dinner) to discuss how things are going. The meeting can be formal or casual.

For formal meetings nominate chairperson to help the family move through the agenda. Most children are capable of this and adore it. In fact, your kids are likely to surprise you with the skills they've already learned at school when it comes to running and contributing to meetings. Young chairpersons and secretaries will of course need your support. Ideally, rotate these positions at each meeting if you plan to take the formal route.

Younger children always want their say straightaway, especially when they get excited. To reduce chaos, have the speaker hold a talking piece. This might be a teddy bear, a soft foam ball or whatever is agreed on. The rule is that only the person holding the item can speak.

Consciously divide each family meeting into two parts;

Part one:

This is when we purposely breathe life into one or more of your Family Mission Statements. If, for example, 'kindness and helping one another' is on your Mission Statement, begin by mentioning when you've witnessed someone being 'kind or helpful'. Ask each person to acknowledge a time when someone was 'kind or helpful' to them. The fact is that it's very powerful for kids to know that the adults have noticed some of their best efforts; it creates a good feeling and makes everyone want to pull together!

Don't shy away from mentioning when your own behaviour wasn't the best. Share your mistakes because it helps kids to discover that you make them too! Allow your children

to witness you modelling honesty and regret. This is perhaps some of the most empowering modelling grownups can do for kids. Let them see you set a new goal and make a commitment to improve. This gives others the courage to be honest about their mistakes. Remember, everything about your child's development is a work in progress.

Part two

This part of the meeting concerns discussion points. Why not create an agenda in advance? One idea is to keep the agenda on the fridge or pin-up board. Remind the kids to add one or two things they want to raise. By doing this, the family meeting takes on a structure that everyone knows about in advance. Resist the urge to put too much on the agenda. And, resist the urge to let this part of the meeting dominate.

When someone raises an issue or has a complaint, the procedure is that they must also suggest a possible win/ win solution. Even though you may be keen to point out what the kids are not doing well, temper your impulse to binge on the negatives. Family meetings work best with a focus on strengths and solutions, so show the kids how you remain hopeful and positive, even when discussing the tough issues.

When it comes to making decisions - especially making rules - work through consensus rather than a majority vote. Majority votes nearly always leave someone feeling as though they have lost. If consensus can't be reached after an energetic discussion then put it off until the next day or the next meeting. Our suggestion is that when you negotiate a new rule or expectation with your kids, you try to load it in their favour. By working in this way children

experience that through discussion, listening and negotiation, they have a voice and can institute change.

End the meeting by choosing a favourite snack for everyone, having dessert or playing a game together. Simple circle games like pass the smile or pass the high-5 work well.

The spirit of family meetings are to review what's happening, to revel in what's working well (remember - catching positive behaviours best influences the changes you want), to discuss changes, make compromise and set new directions. So often it's not making the 'rule' that makes a difference, but the act of engaging your kids in the participation.

Family Rules (or values)

Why have rules? What good are they? Rules help to keep each of us safe, sociable and responsible for what we do. They highlight how-to treat and live with one another by delivering expectations, structure and predictability. When developed

logically and good-naturedly with children, rules assist us from becoming overbearing or from constantly overreacting to irritating incidents. This in turn strengthens the emotional steadiness within the family - the very essence of raising mentally healthy young people.

Begin by putting to your children, no matter their age, the question; "What rules do you think will help our family live well together?" Just as you know what is likely to help, so will the kids.

Have your Family Mission Statement in front of you, and draw ideas from it;

EXAMPLE: 'Family Mission Statement'

— Our family values truth and trust
— We encourage each other
— Our kindness glues us together
— We listen to each other and respect each person's thoughts and efforts
— We show responsibility by trying to fix our mistakes

EXAMPLE: 'Family Rules' to emerge from the 'Family Mission Statement' above

— We tell the truth
— We are kind to each other
— We listen and are helpful
— We fix the mistakes we make

Are you surprised that there are so few rules? Most are. Just three or four positively crafted rules will do the trick!

The intention is not to imprison kids with a list of severe rules that cover every possible contingency. Instead, our aim is to gently persist at highlighting how healthy families treat and live with one another. This is a work in progress, and to be effective, parents have to talk between themselves about what is important before they share with their children. If one of you tends to be more autocratic than the other, then allow the more conciliatory partner to lead the meetings. As you are fast seeing, the process (keeping the kids involved) holds the greatest value. And naturally, rules are easier to raise, to negotiate and stick with when there is a history of listening to one another and resolving issues through discussion. Start the process now! It's never too late.

A family motto

Mottos and sayings have been a part of family life for centuries. Usually, it's a phrase or sentence that captures the Family's Mission Statement or condenses what matters to them. It can be playful, profound, even in code - it doesn't matter - so long as your family knows what it means and finds value in it. Here are some ideas to build from;

- Family first
- Always there to care
- Happiness - that's a good life!
- The best part of a problem is finding the solution together
- Hansberrys stick together
- Le Messuriers never give up
- Attitude is everything
- our job is to pick the best one
- We aren't perfect, but together we can do anything
- What good have I done today?
- Who have we helped today?

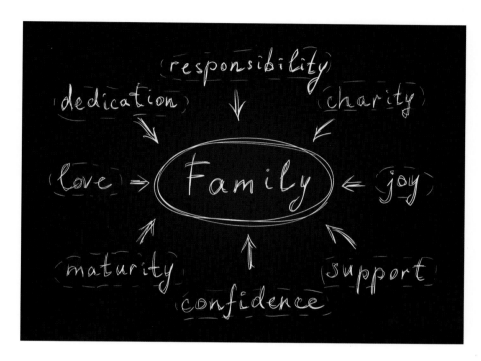

A Family Motto is the sort of thing likely to stay with a child forever. The trick is to reinforce the Family Motto is by living it, and being honest about ourselves and our actions at Family Meetings.

Once you've created your Family Mission Statement, rules and motto, print them, date them and have everyone sign off on them. Display them proudly so they can be seen and used as a reference. Schedule that every six to twelve months you revise your mission statement, rules and motto. These need to grow with your family. So, with some new possibilities in mind, let's take a look at how the bean bag disaster from the beginning of this chapter may have been handled differently if a 'family mission statement' and 'family meetings' were an enduring part of the mix.

Chapter 1:
Rules

Act 1, "It wasn't us, mum" - replayed

Mum *(Exasperated, red faced and poised to jump into lecture mode)*
"Oh… I can't believe this. What were you thinking?

(Mum stops, breathes deeply for a moment and checks her own emotions. The kids find her silence unnerving and feel uncomfortable)

Alex *(breaks the awkward silence)*
"Well, Dotty started throwing…"

Dotty
"Ohhhhhhh, I…"

Mum *(holding a finger to her lips and almost whispering)*
"Shhhhh! Blaming one another won't get this mess cleaned up."

(Silence again as Mum deliberately slows things down)

Mum
"What do our family rules say about how we treat each other and our belongings?"

Abby
"That we respect each other and our belongings."

Mum
"That's right." *(Mum eyeballs each of the kids and they shoot back a knowing glance)*. "So, what happens now?"

Ross
"We clean up the mess?"

(As Ross provides a direction, calm sweeps across the kids and the need to blame one another passes)

Abby
"I'll get the vacuum cleaner."

Mum
"Abby, I think you'll all need to drop to the floor and pick up as many as you can before subjecting my poor old vacuum cleaner to the rest, alright?"

(The six of them drop to the floor to work on the mess as mum begins to walk away)

Mum
"We'll talk about this at an emergency family meeting tonight when Dad's home. For now, clean up, help each other and think of a sensible way to replace my beanbag and help my disappointment."

My Notes:

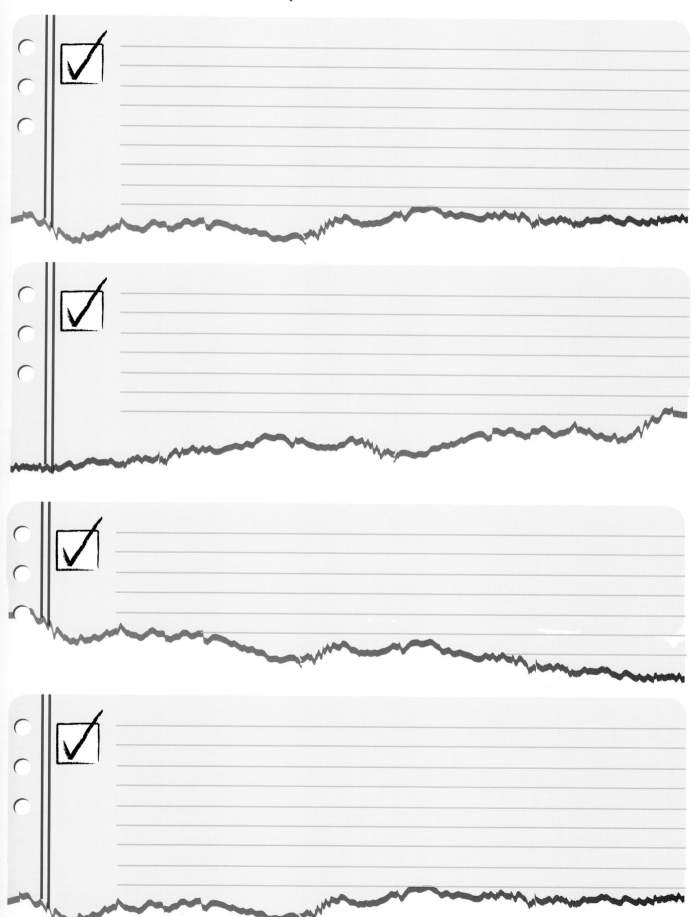

Chapter 2:

How-to catch and build positive behaviours

Recipe rescue:

ideas to avoid 'boil overs' and build your children's positive behaviours

The scenario:

Mum, dad and their two kids are at a large gathering with friends. They have two kids; Adam 10 and Marko 6. Here's a commentary of dad's comments to Marko throughout the afternoon… "I've just told you, Marko. Don't interrupt", "Don't touch that. Put it back - you know better", "Put that down", "Marko, leave it alone", "Leave me alone", "Go and do something - anything!", "You're driving me crazy", "That's silly", "That's so naughty, Marko", "If you don't stop we're going home".

Later, at home, dad asked Marko why he was being so naughty. His response was insightful; "I just wanted some noticement, dad!"

This response gets to the heart of the matter. All of us crave a little 'noticement', or attention, and we all develop behaviours that 'we think' works to get us noticed. Like it or not, we are the main attention dispensers for our kids. Kids crave our attention and it reflects the way in which human beings are designed. Our brains are hard-wired for interaction and we seek attention to create connection and stimulation. We all need attention because having our presence acknowledged indicates that we belong. Being connected and attached to parents is a primary ingredient for an emotionally healthy life.

First, there's some science to be mastered!

Providing our kids with the sort of attention that leads them in positive directions requires an understanding of a little theory. Here it is. You see, 'praise' and 'reprimand' both tick the box for kids to get attention. That's right, many kids will take the attention in whatever package it comes in - being nagged, lectured, yelled at, sooked over, overly attended to or genuinely thanked for cooperative behaviour - it's all good to them! They don't discriminate. Equally, some parents don't discriminate between positive and negative attention giving. They just react without giving thought to the types of behaviour they are really encouraging. When observed from outside, these mistakes are frustratingly obvious to others. Yet, one fact remains; our everyday responses provide our kids with strong, continuous feedback. It is us who encourages our children's behaviour for better or worse. It is us who deliver the message.

Let us explain with these scenarios...

Scenario 1

Frank says in annoyance, "That's it, William, that's plain silly! How many times do I have to ask you? Off to your room for time-out and don't come back until I tell you."

On this occasion, William heads off to his room and reappears in 32 seconds with an impish little look on his face. Even though William is 11 years old that look still melts his father's heart, so William is allowed to return. He continues to seek more and more attention through silliness for the rest of the afternoon. Frank has rewarded William's annoying behaviour and guaranteed it will continue.

Scenario 2

Frank says in annoyance, "That's it, William, that's just silly! How many times do I have to ask you? Off to your room for time-out and don't come back until I tell you."

On this occasion William heads off to his room and reappears in 32 seconds with the usual impish little look on his face. William is 11 years old, and his father feels as though he's too old to keep on trying to get away with 'silly' behaviour by using 'the cutsie routine'. So, in front of guests, Frank 'boils over' at William. William looks crestfallen. Frank eventually stops and the guests squirm uncomfortably. Frank has just rewarded

William's attention seeking behaviour. Deep inside William's psyche, he believes this gala show of words and emotion in front of guests has given him spectacular attention and cemented his position in the family. After all, dad does love him unconditionally! So, William will continue to seek more and more attention in the same kind of way. Frank has rewarded William's annoying behaviour and guaranteed it will continue.

In both scenarios Frank spotted the 'bad habit', but couldn't take the next step; to gradually replace a behaviour that is not working for William with a new, more 'desirable' habit.

Recipe rescue:

the 'art' of giving attention to the behaviours you want!

The art

The starting point for this recipe rescue is to accept our job. Those of us who do well socially, develop behaviours that get us noticed in ways that please others; we're cooperative, responsive, easy going, realistic, kind and show good humour. These socially cohesive behaviours are what we want to encourage in our children. To get this isn't a matter of dragging kids along to a 'child expert' to fix them. The confronting news is that it's actually the parent's behaviour that needs the work. Here's our advice on how to build your children's positive behaviours. In

a nutshell, it means focusing a whole lot more on catching them doing the behaviours we value, and praising them for those positive actions. Giving attention to children is like fertilizing them. The behaviours you give attention to are the behaviours that will grow!

Go slowly, slowly

The truth - every kid is in rehearsal. They are clumsy, learning, gathering experience and bound to make poor judgments, and sometimes they will make very big mistakes! It's what young inexperienced human beings do. They are not in a place to perform exactly how we expect them to behave, perfectly and on cue every time. Mistakes are needed in order to learn and grow. Use mistakes as teachable moments rather than moments to criticise, lecture, humiliate and penalise.

Mimicking is powerful!

What a freaky realisation! Our kids do as we do - they mimic us!
Parents who deliberately live happy, well-connected, emotionally flexible and balanced lives send a message about how to live life to their children. Those poised interactions drip feed a powerful behavioural signal to their children. Their calmness and good-sense exudes confidence and has a positive influence. Alternatively, modelling loss of control, anger, disrespect, gossip and saying damaging things in the heat of the moment teach children to do exactly the same. It's near impossible to help children manage their feelings in healthy ways if they don't consistently see us doing this. They watch our every move. They pick up on how we handle disappointment and conflict, how we enjoy ourselves with friends and how

Chapter 2:

How-to catch and build positive behaviours

our attitudes about people and the world steer our behaviour. What we do is so much more important than what we tell them.

How-to catch 'good' behaviours

When your child is behaving the way you like, be sure to give them some positive feedback. For instance, you might say, "I really like the way you're playing so nicely with Seb. You're helping him to win as well!" This is far more powerful than waiting for something to go wrong and suddenly saying, "Don't do that. Seb's younger than you and needs a chance to win sometimes". When you use positive feedback try to briefly describe the behaviour that you want to see more of. The behavioural experts tell us that we should try to say six to ten positive remarks, or praise, for every negative comment, or tell-off. We think that if you can reach this benchmark you should call the Vatican because you are a serious candidate for sainthood! Seriously, a ratio of two positives to one negative in our experience is a very healthy standard. This keeps things in balance, and particularly keeps our mindset in a positive sphere.

Use mistakes as teachable moments rather than moments to criticise, lecture and penalise

How-to deliver praise

When we're trying to cultivate a new, better behaviour we sometimes overplay praise, like, "Oh, Antonio, you're fantastic! Good, good boy! You're the one - that's just what we want you to do all of the time. That's great, mate. Fantastic! Wow, you did it just like we wanted. You're the best."

Praise like this just isn't sustainable and sounds fake. To be effective praise has to be short, specific and focused. Say how the behaviour is helpful, "Hey Antonio, thanks for getting ready fast. That makes it easy for everyone and we can get going on time. Let's get going."

Fewer words are more powerful and communicate that kids belong through their contributions. Secondly, praise directed at a personal level actually sees kids withdrawing their 'effort' in order to minimize the risk to self. Always try to praise the effort rather than the child personally. Pull right back on saying, "good girl" or "good boy" as this is best for puppy training. Instead say, "You did a good job cleaning your room" or "You made a good decision" or

"Fabulous effort" or "That really helps – thanks". Oh, and avoid a patronising tone. Deliver the praise as you would to a close, intelligent friend.

Praise is priceless. It gives children the idea that we know they can meet expectations. It also lets them know that we're paying attention and are interested.

Tactical ignoring

Tactical ignoring concerns being 'tactical' - it is not about ignoring all of your children's behaviours! It is a strategy to deliberately ignore certain behaviours. By not rewarding these behaviours with our attention they will reduce and gradually disappear. Be warned though - if you're accustomed to buying into most negative things your children do you will find this exhausting to start with. And once the kids sense you aren't noticing what you used to, they'll press harder to restore the model you once used. Be ready for this! So, from time to time, when you've lost energy and perseverance it's okay to run away! Just move to another place. Don't say anything or look irritated. Just go and close a door behind you! The toilet is a good place to hide - it's not an admission of defeat! In fact, you may have just prevented a major setback in tactical ignoring.

Set up a Token Reinforcement System

Human beings behave according to the pleasure principle; behaviour that's rewarding will continue and behaviour that is unrewarding usually stops. A Token Reinforcement System, or a Token Economy, aims to give progressive, positive feedback to kids about what is valued. It establishes a desirable behaviour by 'charting' their success on to something like a traditional 'star chart'. Star charts, or similar, provide a motivating way to help children to stay excited about a goal. Then, as they succeed, they can see their effort nudging them towards the agreed incentive. Token Systems help family life run so much more smoothly!

Ideas build Token Systems:

- **Optimism counts!**
- **Describe the new behaviour**
- **Choose an incentive**
- **Positive parenting**
- **Go visual - track improvements**
- **Different kids, different systems**
- **What's earned is theirs**
- **Build the program out**

Optimism counts!

Earmark a specific behaviour - usually just one at a time - you'd like to see more of. For example, cleaning teeth morning and night, taking turns, sitting at the table during mealtimes, showing kindness, tidying up, staying in bed at night, doing homework or using another strategy or two instead of immediately crying, getting angry or 'blowing up'. Use the idea as a spark to fire-up your child's desire to make a change. Get them on side, even if you have a high powered job and this seems below you!

Describe the new behaviour

Be clear about the new, positive behaviour that you wish to work on together. Help your child to see how they need to look and sound when using this behaviour. One idea is to snap a photo of them performing this behaviour. The photograph can be attached to the 'star chart' or 'tracking sheet' as a reminder of how to do this new behaviour. Also decide on a 'secret signal' as a reminder to stick with the new habit. Discuss this and role-play how to do it before starting the plan.

Choose an incentive

Choose something they wish to earn, and make it highly motivating. Motivating incentives are very, very hard to find for kids who are spoiled - who already have everything, or can get anything when they want it.

Incentives entice your child toward goals you think are best for them, but the ultimate goal is for them to gain self-control. This is not about creating reward addicts. We need to be clever and build the Token System out over time - more on this soon. Oh, by the way, if the term 'reward' or 'incentive' offends your moral high ground then make sure you stop using, ' a fair day's work for a fair day's pay', 'Fly Buy points' and 'loyalty cards' for yourself. It's exactly the same thing.

Positive parenting

Success depends on positive parent language and positive attitudes. The reverse is a parent who constantly uses the Token System to threaten and shame their child, saying, "Well, if you don't do this right now there won't be any rewards today!" This is silly and will blow up in your face.

Go visual - track improvements

Traditionally, this is where 'star charts' have been used, but any engaging visual idea to track progress will do. We have included two 'tracking charts' to give you an idea later this chapter. Place the 'tracking chart' where it can be seen - most parents strategically place them on the kitchen table or refrigerator - so it serves as a frequent reminder of the behaviour being chased. As your kids display the targeted behaviour there is a tangible recognition in the form of a symbol or token on the chart. Oh, a wise word; some kids will want it taken down when friends come over!

Different kids, different systems

Young children respond best to immediate feedback for using their new thinking. This helps keep the motivation alive! A consistent drip-feed is better than, "if you're good all week, you can have a reward". When did that last work for a five-year-old?

Older children are able to respond to more complicated systems which have longer delays built in before they achieve the incentive.

What's earned is theirs

Anything your child has worked for and earned remains theirs – it cannot be taken away. When your child relapses to the old unwanted behaviour and chooses to ignore reminders or secret signals to help get them back on track, a simple consequence is given - time out, early to bed or the loss of a privilege. This is real life at work. At this point it will simply take your child longer to achieve the incentive. Your role here is to allow for a restart without the undertone of failure or loss of dignity.

Build the program out

Once the incentive is achieved, celebrate! The next step is to set up a new Token System and gently raise the bar. This is called 'building the program out'. So next time around you might continue to target the same positive behaviour, and add a new one to it. Now is the time to introduce a few more steps for your child to reach the new incentive. Never hesitate to change the physical appearance of the tracking sheet as this adds interest! Remember that we are not chasing perfection. This is all about normalising behaviours.

Token Reinforcement Systems work because they help kids, and parents, get over the hump of switching off an undesirable behaviour and replacing it with a better one. They are interactive and fun too. Here are a few examples of Token Reinforcement Systems.

Token Reinforcement Systems

'YES JARS'

Buy a large plastic jar for each of your kids. Have them decorate the jar with their name on it. Every so often, perhaps once or twice a week put coloured plastic tokens on the bench next to the jars (each child can have their own colour). Tell your children that during this hour you want to see smiles, hear "Yes, mum" or "Yes, dad" and witness cooperative behaviours. Promise that each time you see a positive response you'll get them to place a token in their jar. Then, at the end of the hour they add up the number of tokens they've received. Set up a menu that boldly shows them what 5 or 10 or 30 tokens can purchase. Allow your kids to save tokens from one time to the next so they can earn the more impressive incentives.

Avoid overplaying your hand; tokens earned should never be removed if things happen to go badly.
The other variation to this is to use raffle tickets. Then, at the end of the allocated time a raffle is drawn. The more tickets a child has increases their chances of winning! This practice is pure fun and recognises their persistence.

Happy/Sad face grids

The 'Happy and Sad face grid' aims at reinforcing helpful and thoughtful behaviours. To start, draw up a grid of 10 or 15 squares on an A4 sheet of paper, place your child's name on it and buy a roll of happy and sad faced stickers ready to use. Display the grid in a prominent place; on the pin-up board or the dinner table. Agree on a specific positive behaviour you want to see more of. Every time you see it, attach a happy face to the grid. However, when there's a "no", outright refusal and they won't budge, a sad face is calmly placed onto the grid. At the end of the allotted time count up the number of happy and sad faces. If there are more happy faces than sad faces on a grid, then the owner of that grid receives the predetermined incentive. It's an easy method and can be varied to suit the behaviour you are looking for.

Star Charts

Here's an idea used by one of our resourceful families. They have two girls, delightful and strikingly strong willed, around middle primary school age. When either of the girls achieve their star chart objective - completing chores, being ready for school on time, getting ready for bed independently, happily taking a shower, tidying up the bedroom, putting away toys, remembering to clean teeth, and so on - their parents organise a family day or half day that involves visiting a series of surprise places. The 'magical mystery tours' are always joyful and these parents are certain that this idea, brimming with anticipation, provides them with loads of leverage towards influencing the girls' more desirable behaviours.

Cut Ups

To encourage her son to develop a new behaviour, one mum agreed to deliver a new DS game, computer game or DVD when he met a behavioural goal they set together (these things were of course very, very important to him). Here's the thing, and it's clever; she bought the item, photocopied the cover and cut it into 15 pieces just like a jigsaw. They agreed that he could have it when he'd earned each of the pieces for achieving a new targeted behaviour, bit by bit. Clever, eh?

A Bright Idea!

Alexis was a tricky to manage 10 year old. Her moodiness, especially around dinner time, was often awful. Once at the table her mood simmered and it wouldn't be long before she made an offensive remark about the food, her day or a family member. Very quickly she'd find a reason for not wanting to eat. Family tension intensified as parents played right into her hands and rewarded her negative behaviour with more and more attention; voices became raised, and Alexis would eat a few morsels at her parent's insistence.

To improve the dinner time climate Alexis' parents used a Token Reinforcement System. As she sat down for dinner with her parents, she would light a small tea candle set on the table. The idea was that for each tea candle that burnt away, Alexis could receive 6 music downloads for her iPod. And, this was the only way she had access to music. Suddenly, there was a great incentive to keep the candle burning! Using this system the candle would be blown out as soon as Alexis fell back into her old grumpy or sulky way. As soon as she apologised the candle was lit again. As Alexis was mindful of the candle burning, she spent more time at the table eating and positively relating to her family. Once she had eaten she would blow out the candle and leave the table.

This approach redirected Alexis' habitual negative dinner time talk into far more optimistic conversations and responses.

iRewardChart

iRewardChart is an iPhone application that helps kids to stay on track with behaviour using a Token Reinforcement approach. Go to *http://www.youtube.com/watch?v=HJFELXE-y5E* to see how it works. Basically, this 'app' motivates kids to achieve agreed behaviours in return for incentives (e.g. 10 stars will earn a trip to the movies). Each day a child has a chance to earn a star by doing the predetermined activity, chore or task. It might be to tidy up their bedroom and straighten their quilt, and when they do this they receive a star. You may add as many tasks, and children, as you want. Children also have the option of earning more than one star for additional activities or if they did a great good job. Any stars previously earned remain theirs no matter what, even if they have had a bad, bad day. The 'app' has lock ability. By entering a simple code only you can give the stars! iRewardChart also keeps track of the data so you can see the improvements in your child's helpful behaviour.

Chore Pad

Chore Pad is another useful application for iPhones and iPads. It is easy to use and applies the Token Reinforcement System similar to the iRewardChart. Go to *http://www.youtube.com/watch?v=8Jlr1PBYY6Y&feature=related* to learn how it works.

Basically, you insert the name of each child and add their photo to personalise their chart. The idea is to log in the everyday chores for each child so they can be ticked off as they're done throughout the week. As this happens, gold stars and trophies accumulate. Kids can see weekly progress at a glance. You can also enter rewards which can eventually be redeemed in exchange for the gold stars and trophies. The parents who use it tell us that it's a wonderful way to keep track of chores and keeps their kids motivated!

A point system

Eleven year old Louis and his mum devised a point system which inspired him to contribute more around the house. Each day Louis could earn 1 point for feeding the dog, 1 point for making his bed, 2 points for stacking the dishwasher, 2 points for picking up the doggy doo and 2 points for taking out the recyclables. Dianne and Louis decided on a formula to convert points to dollars, and for his first incentive Louis chose a special edition hard covered Star Wars book. But, Diane was clever. She deliberately whetted his appetite with a brief visit to the bookstore. It provided a moment for Louis to hold the book, flick pages and smell the new ink. Oh yes, it set the scene for a successful outcome. In the ensuing weeks Dianne was happy to prompt Louis, but the beauty of their simple system was the way it dramatically reduced his resistance. It was a win/win solution.

Ingredients:

- A child not doing what you want them to do
- The consequence of a child making a bad choice
- A fed up parent
- High tension
- A parent trying to act responsibly
- A parent recovering their 'power'
- A child feeling their dignity is threatened
- A history of threats

Recipe rescue:

so you never have to threaten, nag or go on and on

The Scenarios:

Arguments, threats, eruptions and all things ugly

"Tom, for the third time, just take the bloody rubbish out! I'm over you."

"Do the rubbish now or your iPad will join your DS and laptop in the cupboard! Soon you'll have nothing left."

"Maddie, hurry up and get ready for school! What? Why haven't you done your teeth? Where's your other sock? You make me so angry! What's wrong with you? You're driving me mad."

"Jacinta, we've already discussed it. I'm not talking about it anymore!
No, you can't go to Katie's today. Stop going on and on about it!
Don't you tell me to stop going on about it, if you keep arguing I'll do something you'll regret for a long, long time!"

"Raeph, all I want you to do is tidy your bedroom.
Mate, if you want to fight over this then watch me win, because I will. I'll show you how to squash the enemy!"

QUESTION

Does threatening, nagging and going on and on successfully steer our children's behaviour in the direction we hope for?

ANSWER

No. Threatening, nagging and ranting are very blunt tools. When relied on too often by parents their power is more likely to damage kids and harm relationships. The most valuable shaper of children's behaviour is for them to hear genuine praise when they are doing well. This alerts them that they are on track and can achieve. It leads kids to feel confident, obliging, malleable and attached to parents.

Nonetheless, every so often it is natural for all kids to make poor choices or be disobedient, naughty or defiant. What then? What's the best approach? Welcome; this is the essence of our Recipe rescue.

Recipe rescue:

so you never have to threaten, nag or go on and on

There's a much better way than defending your position by arguing, raving on or lecturing the kids about how they should care or be more responsible. By the time something has gone wrong all kids, even littlies, know why things haven't turned out well. Most can even tell you what would have been a better way to deal with it. In this moment of tension, our children don't hear our wisdom or frustration. What they hear is mum or dad over-reacting yet again - "blah, blah, blah …" At this point, already accustomed to our tell-off, their self-protection mechanism locks them into 'parent deaf' mode.

So please, spare your moralising, lecturing and anger - it won't help. The truth is that teaching our kids how to be considerate, social and responsible is a twenty year project, and it demands our consistency. From now on, when your child makes a poor choice, link what you do to these effective ideas. If you do, you'll rarely end up screaming at the kids in order to 'have the last say'. Instead, you'll ensure a healthier connection between their poor choice and a sensible outcome.

Negative, nagging cycles

In reflective moments it's easy to see that the steadiness, care and cooperation we desire from our kids is heavily linked to how we feel. Parenting is seriously relentless work, so it's easy to feel tired and fed up, and fall into negative cycles.

"Hurry up!"
"Watch where you're walking!"
"Why did you do that?"
"How many times do I have to tell you?"
"Can't you do anything right?"
"Why don't you listen?"

Nagging destroys trust, confidence and respect. It will make some kids nervy and motivate others to be oppositional and reactive. Trust us - that's the truth!

Get some hard data

If you feel you are stuck in a negative style of thinking and a negative tone when you speak to the kids, and you'd like to switch from it, trial this as a way to gather some hard data. Start to record your child's behaviour on a calendar! Keep this for your private use. Use a red, yellow and green coloured coding system. At the end of each day colour that day's square on the calendar with one of the colours. Red on the days your child has completely refused to cooperate or negotiate. Yellow to show the days when there has been a conflict, but in the end a reasonable compromise was found. Yellow is encouraging because we're always looking for opportunities to negotiate, compromise and find solutions.

Warning: although compromise is a sound strategy, it does not eliminate your parental right to make the final decision when it really counts. Lastly, use green for the 'nice n easy' days.

What do you think parents usually find? Less red days than anticipated! They say it 'feels' as though they have far more battles with their kids than they thought. The other discovery is that it if you're not challenging your kids, and they're not challenging you a couple of times a week, then you're not fully engaged as a parent

Managing tricky kid behaviour

Managing our own emotion is hard enough, so it's no surprise to discover that managing the volatile emotion and sometimes willful behaviour of kids takes real skill, self-discipline and class. Often we know how to redirect our child's behaviour in theory, but stumble at the very moment we find ourselves under pressure. Our theoretical skills desert us! Practice does help. The best idea is to try building your new skills by taking small steps, just one at a time. Here's the 'art' to better manage tricky kid behaviour –

Chapter 3:
The 'art' of managing tricky kid behaviour

Choose your battles wisely

Be a clever tactical ignorer and allow 90% of your child's annoying behaviours to slip by. Only pick up on the 10% that really matter. As you switch your attention to what really matters, instead of nit-picking *too much too often,* your reactions are far less likely to reward your child's negative attention-seeking behaviours. Tactical ignoring is about ignoring unimportant misbehavior - it is not about ignoring your child and all of their behaviour. Hindsight tells us that so many childish behaviours drop out with maturity. Yet, a few parents who have the same rigid traits as their child fail to see this obvious choice. These poor souls will not shift their pattern of tight control parenting, and the power struggle always wreaks serious relational damage.

When problem behaviour arises, stop!

That's right; actually stop what you are doing. Move toward your child and check in with yourself about how you are feeling. If you're feeling annoyed, allow this flush of emotion to pass. You need to look composed and resourceful.

As one of our thirteen year old clients said to his mother, "Don't tell me not to be a psycho while you're acting like one!" When a child is struggling with their emotion the last thing that will help is an out-of-control adult.

Be calm, controlled and deliberate

Look at them and use a calm, measured voice. Use the child's name and briefly state the difficulty.

- For younger children, give a clear choice what will fix the problem, and direct them to do it.
- For older children, tell them they'll need to make a 'good choice' to fix the problem.

* In both cases, state the negative consequence you'll use if they choose not to make their best choice. Use as few words as possible, *"Lawson… turn it off now or there will be no IPod touch tomorrow."*

Encourage them to make a good choice

At this point deliberately encourage them to make their best choice. Help them come out of the interaction with their dignity intact. With a sudden loss of dignity - when kids feel completely defeated by us - they will say and do things that are awfully out of character. Occasionally, when you sense the timing is right, do the unexpected. Perhaps, take the wind out of their sails by using humour. Many a situation can be rescued with a wink, silly face,

poked out tongue, dare, joke, zombie walk, friendly eye roll, thumbs-up, kind comment or by simply changing the subject. Be practical and tactical - be truly adult!

Move away

Walking away stops us from standing over our kids demanding instant reform – this can be a recipe for disaster with kids who take time to process information or have to win. In extreme circumstances, they'll explode, saying, "You don't know me" or "I don't care about you or your stupid consequences! Nothing you can do will change it." Never bite back. Instead, say something like:

"I love you way too much to argue about this"
"Well that's the way it's going to be, so think wisely" … and walk away
"Buddy / Sweetheart, I'm not arguing with you about this"… and walk away

What's absolutely critical is how you use your voice. Try not to sound righteous, or like you are their opponent because this is not a situation you are trying to win. You are respectfully telling your kids that you are choosing not to argue with them.

Negative consequences

Negative consequences include; the loss of a privilege, missing out on something, time alone which offers respite to all, early to bed, apologising or writing an apology, repairing damage, taking on additional chores and so on. For most primary aged children the negative consequence should be applied the same day the problem occurred. We do not recommend heavy handed consequences that continue for days. Negative consequences should be used sparingly and always followed through, otherwise we teach kids to ignore and to disregard. The same applies for adolescents, but it needs to be tweaked

When a child is struggling with their emotion the last thing that will help is an out-of-control adult.

a little. For example, you might offer your young teen a wise word, state your opinion and then back off. Then, let the outcome play out. If they make a poor choice then be sure to be helpful, and not capitalise on their error as a chance to gloat, or to say, "I told you so...."

Never double up on consequences

In a situation, where your child persists with the problem behaviour, tell them there will be a consequence and name it. Then, walk away without another word even if they up the ante and their behaviour deteriorates. Tactically ignore almost anything they say or do next - don't buy into it. Later, you must follow through with the one negative consequence you first stated. Kids, just like us, learn best through experiencing both positive and negative consequences connected to their behaviour, so it is worth your while to perfect how well you go about this.

Praise

Praise your child when they respond positively. No need to 'throw a party' or act as though your child has done you a favour, just acknowledge their wise choice and move on. And don't forget - from time to time - spontaneously offer a positive reinforcement (a reward or incentive) to highlight their positive response. "Hey, you were so helpful at shopping today, let's celebrate with ice cream."

Persistence

Finally, keep persisting with this code when you have to manage tricky kid behaviour. This is not a perfect remedy, and you will have your slip ups as you try these new management skills, but these approaches are logical, safe and should reduce emotional explosiveness. The earlier the code is embraced the easier it becomes for everybody. Your consistency over the long term, more than anything, will determine the effectiveness.

Finally, we have a golden piece of advice worth inscribing on to your psyche -

From now on when you find yourself in conflict with any of your kids, do this. Try and react to it in the same way you'd treat the child of your most precious friend who has just made this very same poor judgement. Do you see the link? You can still be disappointed, authoritive and decisive, but this attitude avoids hostility, aggressiveness, revenge and occasional spitefulness.

As you use this approach your children are far more likely to see the crystal clear links between choice and outcome. You plant a life lesson - take responsibility for your own behaviour. And, whatever you do, avoid power struggles and extreme emotions. They will happen from time to time, but sidestep them as often as you can because they bring no good to your relationship and to your family whatsoever.

Recipe rescue:

steering sibling conflict in positive directions

Ingredients:

- **Kids learning how to live with others**
- **Kids who are tired, hungry or seeking stimulation**
- **Kids who've spent too long together**
- **A parent who reacts to, and referees their kids' every squabble**
- **A parent who pays a lot of attention to the kids when they argue**
- **Parents who openly compare their kids**
- **Parents who encourage kids to compete against one another**
- **Kids who've learnt to manipulate their parents to get attention**
- **Parents who don't have a plan to deal with day to day sibling disputes**

The scenarios...

Guarding the remote

The scream from the playroom cuts through the air as eight year old Patrick launches himself into the kitchen, screaming, "He hit me."

Mum storms off to find eleven year old Dawson, sitting in the beanbag guarding the TV remote on his lap. Dawson shoots her a glance and says, "He snatched it from me. I had it first."

Monica snaps and grabs the remote and removes the batteries from the back.

"Now nobody gets the TV. The both of you can live without it for a week!" *'God knows how I'll make that work,'* she thinks to herself.

Lego wars

"Dad, she's stolen the Lego from my Imperial Cruiser for her stupid Barbie house."

"It's not stupid," replies Macey.

"It's not your Lego," Stefan calls as he runs towards Macey's bedroom. She gives chase.

"Stefan, stop," dad calls from the kitchen. Stefan quickly destroys the Barbie house as Macey tries to stop him.

"Stefan, what are you doing?" dad calls as he closes in.

"I'm just taking my Lego back," Stefan says with a snigger. Macey is in tears. Stefan continues.

Peter finally arrives, "Stefan that was unkind."

Stefan grins and is having way too much fun to stop.

An X-wing Star fighter

Caleb proudly shows his mum what he made at school.

"I made it myself. I got everything from the making box. It's an X-wing Star fighter," he boasts.

Eight year old Anna, Caleb's sister, snorts, "That nothing like an X-wing." Caleb's pride plummets like a pricked balloon. Mum turns on Anna, "That's mean! Who made you the expert on Star Wars anyway, young lady?" Anna, up to every challenge, bounces right back. "Mum, no one does Star Wars anymore!"

Mum kneels down to sooth Caleb. "Don't worry about her. I think it's a beauty."

Anna flounces out of the kitchen.

Competition between siblings has occurred since the beginning of time as kids vie for time, attention, love, resources and approval from their parents. It's not new! Time travel back to the biblical story of Cain and Abel; it tells of Cain's awful jealousy after God appeared to favour his brother. His competiveness and jealousy eventually lead him to murder Abel. Many of Shakespeare's plays were tangled around sibling rivalry because it sets an intriguing backdrop of one-upmanship, scheming and deception. You may recall Kate and Bianca fighting bitterly in The Taming of the Shrew as they strived for their father's attention. Who'll ever forget the sibling rivalry on the Simpsons between troublemaker, Bart Simpson and his nerdy sister, Lisa? What about the ongoing rivalry in the context of healthy connections between the brothers and sisters in sitcoms as, Everybody Loves Raymond, Frasier, Brothers and Sisters and Parenthood?

Sibling relationships are the longest lasting and most constant intimate relationships formed by human beings - and mostly, they are driven by love. They last longer than most friendships, through the deaths of parents and beyond many, many marriages. Sharing an extended shared history from early childhood into old age is significant!

Sibling rivalry

the most incredible preparation for life

Arguments and fights between siblings are normal, even though they can be irritating. If you grew up with siblings you'd remember the annoyances; sharing bedrooms, bathrooms, shampoo, back seats in cars, television, toys, games, friends and the attention of your parents. It isn't easy; most of us have memories of frayed tempers, injustices and some favouritism.

Without realising it at the time, what you and your siblings were doing was the most incredible life preparation. In the relative safety of your own home you were practicing how to deal with highly competitive feelings; love, loyalty, anger, conflict and forgiveness. This interaction was powerful in shaping your identity; how you fitted in, how the family defined you and ultimately how you saw yourself.

The mistakes you made with your sibling(s) were an important part of the learning you took from home into your relationships with workmates, partners and your own kids.

There's good news here! The research and our experience tells us that siblings who squabbled with one another as kids likely ended up better friends as adults.

Competitive or collaborative?

Many of the upsets between siblings result from natural competitive feelings. The scene for competitive tension is set as soon as the second child arrives and the first-born is de-throned! No longer is the first child the centre of the universe. Their universe suddenly becomes a shared one, and 'number two' can easily be viewed as a threat! From the moment two kids (or more) must share, the stage is set for one of two broad cultures to emerge: a culture of competition or a culture of collaboration.

The way parents speak to kids, speak about kids, share time with them, address conflict, correct behaviour, reward, celebrate and discipline drip feeds powerful messages to kids about how they 'belong' in the family. It is us who determines whether home becomes every man for himself, or becomes a place where we lift each other up. The answers to the questions overleaf will provide some indicators about what's happening in your home.

Sibling Culture Survey

Let's determine the sibling culture at your place. Is it competitive or collaborative?

Ratings:
1 = rarely/ no, **2** = sometimes/ a bit, **3** = frequently/ a lot, **4** = always/ yes
Record 1 or 2 or 3 or 4 next to each question and then total them up

Do your kids squabble a lot?	
Do your kids quarrel more in your company for your benefit?	
Do they argue in front of one parent more than the other?	
When you interfere in their bickering do they instantly begin to blame one another?	
Is there a big difference in the kid's behaviour when you compare how they behave at home together, to when they stay over together at a friends or relation's home?	
Do the kids seem to get along with other kids better than they get along with each other?	
Does it feel like the kids fight all of the time?	
Do the kids constantly rub against each other so that a blow-up is never far away?	
Are you more likely to hear the kids saying unkind words to each other, like; "You're stupid", "You'll never get it", "Is that the best you can do?" "Cry baby!" or "You're such a loser?"	
Are your kids highly protective of their belongings and won't share them with one another?	
How do the kids respond when their brother or sister has a win or finds some success; are they more likely to make jealous or spiteful remarks?	
Do the kids tell you, with glee, when their brother or sister has made a mistake, or is in trouble?	
When a sibling is having a bad moment or a bad day, does the other one transform into a perfect angel?	
When one of you children has a friend over to play is the other one angling to 'take over', 'annoy' or 'sabotage' the experience?	

Total: _____

Scoring guide:
Highly competitive – 45 or above
Competitive – 35 to 45
Collaborative – 25 to 35
Highly Collaborative – below 25

How did you go?

Is the 'sibling culture' you've created at home competitive or collaborative?
Whatever your score, don't despair. Every situation is salvageable if you want to put in the work.

As you're probably realising, you are a big part of the reason why the current culture between siblings exists. Just 'tune in' to the ideas in Recipe rescue below, and if you live with a partner, be prepared to have some conversations about forging a plan to build a healthier sibling culture. The road to better days requires a united approach. Kids, who've learned to argue, deflect responsibility and to blame brothers and sisters, know how to work the differences between the two of you. You are actually creating the wiggle room! And, if the results from the survey suggest that the sibling culture in your home is mainly collaborative, then use the Recipe rescue as a checklist to ensure sibling rivalry remains within emotionally healthy limits.

Recipe rescue:

steering sibling conflict in positive directions

Setting limits

As a parent, what can you do to ensure the rivalry between your kids stays within healthy limits?
Let the fighting between your kids run too far, too fast, too often and unchecked, and you may end up with an abusive sibling situation. This is when one child takes complete dominance over a brother or sister. 'Sibling abuse' comes in many forms; physical (repetitive pushing, punching, pinching, gouging, hitting, slapping, biting, hair pulling and choking), emotional (repetitive teasing, name calling, belittling, ridiculing, intimidating and provoking) or sexual (unwanted and inappropriate touching, indecent exposure, intercourse and rape). What an abusive sibling does to their brother or sister inside the family would be called assault outside the family. Indeed, a study by Brigham Young University professor Laura Padilla-Walker found continuing and elevated hostility between siblings is associated with greater risk of delinquency (Padilla-Walker, 2012).
On the other hand, let's not kid ourselves that competition and conflict between kids in the home shouldn't exist. Of course it does and will - our

kids are young, inexperienced and often find themselves competing for the same things because their developmental needs are so similar. It's the way it is. Our role is to monitor their state of interaction and guide them, without obsessively 'over-umpiring' their every move. Yes, there's a tricky line to be walked by parents, and those who do it reasonably well offer siblings a wonderful gift for the future.

We know from intriguing research that there are special gifts that siblings give to one another. Apparently, little sisters tend to safeguard big sisters from depression (Padilla-Walker, 2010). Believe it or not, there's something about having a little sister that makes girls in the ten to fourteen year old group less likely to feel down in the dumps! This same study found that having a loving sibling, either gender, promoted good deeds such as helping others or watching out for other kids. In fact, loving siblings foster helpful attitudes twice as effectively than loving parents can engineer. The message is to encourage sibling affection, because once they arrive at adolescence, it is a big protective factor.

Comparing kids is a disastrous practice

"I wish you'd be more like your sister/brother!"
"Your sister/brother always does it! Why can't you?"
"Mark, I wish you were more like Bill"
"You could try a bit harder and get better grades at school like Bill"
"Thank goodness I don't have to put up with this from Bill!"

Did you hear similar statements as a child from your parents? Was there a brother or sister you had to live up to? Then you don't need us to tell you how such statements discouraged you, stirred up resentment or even inspired jealousy. Comparing kids is downright harmful. It won't make one child try harder. Instead, it sets the scene for point scoring between them. Eventually, one of the kids will arrive at the conclusion, "if I can't be valued for me, then the best way to belong is to get the most attention - I can be the loudest, the most demanding, the most outspoken, the saddest or depressed."

Chapter 4:
Sibling rivalry

Take off your referee's uniform and throw away the whistle

Sometimes kids look as though they're spoiling for a fight, but this isn't the goal at all. Their aim is to generate a basic level of stimulation between one another - in a strange way they are bonding - and there's no more to it than this! The problem is that it's easy for this niggling behaviour to deteriorate into fighting.

Knowing this, parents often blow the whistle and dive headlong into umpiring simply to stop the noise and restore harmony. In reality, once we insert ourselves into the fracas, the goal immediately changes for the kids. Rather than winding one another up, or fighting for the best spot on the couch or in the car, or first on the computer, the kids forget about finding a solution. Instead, now that they have mum or dad's undivided attention. They become ruthless; shout, argue, blame, and twist events to win and prove who really is mum or dad's favourite at the time.

Consider two ideas;

1. Only get involved if your effort is part of a strategic plan.
2. Try not to look and sound overly involved when you must get involved.

So next time, as you see the kids going at one another, deliberately hold back. Step out of your umpiring uniform, throw away the whistle, observe and think far more strategically. Think; is it wiser to ignore this behaviour? Does the behaviour really matter anyway? Do I need to buy into this? If you must buy into it then calmly assert yourself;

"Hey, you two… separate! Now!"
"Hey, if you want to fight, take it outside!"
"You know this won't end well. It's time to walk away from each other!"
"It's not worth it. Someone will end up hurt."

Then, walk away and busy yourself with anything, except the kids!

If the kids momentarily stop say, *"Hey, I knew you could deal with this. I'm proud of you."* Then, return to the task you were occupied with. When they realise that you are not going to mount your steed and gallop in as the white knight of justice to solve their every dispute they'll pick up on two themes;

- You provide a very low level of attention when they fight.

- You have faith in them, and expect them to settle their own disputes.

When the kids decide to fix a row, even if the solution isn't as slick as yours, make sure you give them the attention they truly deserve, say;
"Gee, you guys are growing up. Well sorted."
"I knew you could sort that out, let's celebrate with an ice block."
"That's worth a high five you two. I'm proud of your thinking!"
"Whoa! That was a clever way to manage your feelings."
"You both kept your cool and sorted it! Later we'll go down and hire a DVD to watch together."
"James, I like the way you decided to let Matt go first. That was a great decision and showed that you're too clever to need to win all the time!"

And, continue to check yourself with this question; 'Did praising the kids for solving the quarrel give them better quality attention than telling them off?'

What about when you must step in

Occasionally, you must step in because there's imminent danger or harm to a child. When you must step in there are some healthy ideas to keep in mind;

While we look for, and even manipulate opportunities for children to resolve their own problems, we have to be aware that developmental and temperamental differences between them can sometimes translate into massive power inequalities. One child may be physically stronger, be more reactive or aggressive, be a quicker thinker and be more adept a delivering spiteful words. And, the stronger may not necessarily be the oldest!

The real challenge here is to consistently interact with the kids and observe how they relate with one another. The intimacy that you build is the best protective factor to guard against 'sibling abuse'. When difficulties between siblings prevent living together normally, or become harmful or dangerous, you must get involved. If you suspect that one of your children is being mistreated then take them aside. Talk privately at length, calmly and amicably. Don't try to immediately get to the bottom of it. Instead, talk about what's happening, why it's happening, how long it's been going on, how they feel about it and what can be done to repair the relationship. Listen, and listen very well.

Next, take the other aside. Avoid blaming as this is not to time to conduct a 'witch hunt'. Be prepared to listen to them very carefully. Also be prepared to offer authoritive leadership by bringing it to a family meeting. Try to keep everyone's dignity intact, even though mistakes may have been made. Together set new understandings and boundaries, and decide on a way to monitor and review progress. This may also involve sessions with a skilled professional to help the family remain on a healthier trajectory.

What about when one of the kids comes to you upset over a clash they've had with their brother or sister?

When six year old Mila comes running in complaining that her ten year old brother, Judd, slapped her while they were play wrestling on the trampoline, what do we suggest? We see this as a wonderful 'teachable moment' to up-skill the apparent victim. Make sure you make the most of it. We recommend handling it just like her mother does here;

> Mila, I can see that you're hurt. That's a shame. You must feel awful.
>
> No, Mila, I'm not going outside to tell Judd off. I'll deal with him later.
>
> But, what were you thinking? You know Judd. This has happened when you've play-wrestled before and you know when he's getting angry. You know his look and the words he starts to use better than anyone else.
>
> Staying on the trampoline with Judd, after things had gotten angry was a bad decision.
>
> You chose to ignore what was happening.
>
> All you needed to do was to stop and move away from him. You could have slipped quietly inside and told me what was happening. We could have found something for you to do, or for Judd to do. We could have handled it so it helped you both!
>
> Now, let's clean up those tears. And, remember, from now on when things begin to go wrong between you and Judd be clever and quietly move away - talk to me, or dad, or do something else.

A little later, when Judd is alone Mum firmly reminds him that slapping Mila was wrong. She's not interested in rehashing the events and creating a moment where Judd feels as though he must defend himself. Instead, she's quietly assertive, expresses her disappointment and reminds Judd that he's in a family where people never hit. She's of course referring to the family mission statement. Mum then discusses positive options he will use in the future. Mum firmly emphasises that if he does this again there will be a consequence for him. Mum gets up and moves away from Judd allowing him to think without feeling threatened. Before the end of the day Mum will call Judd and Mila together with her to have a chat about what went wrong and how the problem can be fixed.

Chapter 4:

Sibling rivalry

Reflection

Reflection is a 'perfectly timed moment' you create following a sibling spat. Once they've settled, take the kids aside together (Like Mum will with Judd and Milah) or one-by-one and calmly ask them the questions opposite. Listen and resist the temptation to give them your answers or your interpretation. Allow plenty of time for them to think and respond. The act of asking these questions helps kids to develop the social/emotional problem solving parts of their brain. In addition, it gives you a revealing insight into the quality of their thinking, their capacity to learn and ability to resolve conflict.

> What was the problem?
>
> What was your part in it?
>
> What made you decide to…?
>
> How did you feel when…?
>
> How do you think it was for your brother/sister?
>
> How did you try to sort it out?
>
> How did that work?
>
> Do you want to be fighting?
>
> What might fix this problem (if it's still a problem)?
>
> What might you try next time this problem happens?
>
> How can I help?

Modelling - they never stop watching how we do it

Is it okay to for parents to argue in front of the kids?

Traditionally, the popular thinking has been that parents should take their conflicts behind closed doors, so not to scar children for life! As it turns out, hiding conflict from kids isn't healthy for them, or for parents.

Research teaches us that as long as parental bickering doesn't descend into insults, and the conflict is sorted with goodwill and affection, kids feel secure. Over time, their pro-social behaviour is likely to improve (Cummings, 1994). The important thing here is that the kids actually witness parents sorting the issue. When your kids witness you working through conflict respectfully and productively you increase the chances they will pick up these very same behaviours when they

run into problems. If, on the other hand, your kids see you regularly shout and swear at each other, slam doors and become highly emotional when you have problems, they're likely to pick up those same habits as well. Makes sense doesn't it?

Teach kids to recognise and move beyond 'sticking points'

There are times when deadlocks or 'sticking points' between siblings occur. Typically, they happen when both

… when you witness one of the kids conceding or peacemaking, praise them and tell them what they just used is flexible, friendly thinking. It shows that they are growing up, and this kind of behaviour helps to win friends!

believe they are entitled to have it, have won, or to have their way. These moments are challenging and the flare ups can be truly amazing!

How do you navigate around these 'sticking points'?

Firstly, share that these moments happen to each of us in the adult world too, and to get by, we draw on all sorts of peacemaking ways to keep the dignity of one another. Let them know that in the heat of the moment the natural tendency is to dig in, hold ground and try to win. Introduce the idea of backing-down and how to back-down. Later, when you witness one of the kids conceding or peacemaking, praise them and tell them what they just used is flexible, friendly thinking. It shows that they are growing up, and this kind of behaviour helps to win friends!

When all else fails teach the kids how to use 'Rock Paper Scissors', how-to 'flip a coin' and how to make deals or bargains to solve a deadlocks. Sometimes the simplest of strategies are the most effective.

Spend time with each of the kids

Making one-on-one time for each of the kids is insurance that money can't buy. During these emotionally safe moments little things fall out in conversations providing you with continuing 'snapshots' of how each of the kids are feeling, coping with one another and with life.

Bet you're thinking; "how can I do this?" We understand that in a busy home this is tricky for both mums and dads. The wise word… "If you look for time to do something, you'll never find it, but if you make time, you can make it happen" certainly applies here.

Make a date with each of the kids - just once a month to spend a little time with them. If you keep a diary, put it in there as an appointment and stick to it! Treat it with the importance of a business meeting because when you weigh it up, it's actually more important! Arrange experiences with each kid that you know will be enjoyable. Slip out for a milkshake together, go shopping or for a drive, sit in the car and talk or play a game, head off to the movies, go for a picnic lunch, visit your child's favourite place, walk to the playground, hire a movie and watch it together, or take them on a 'magical mystery tour' in the car together.

American civil rights activist, Jesse Jackson, was spot on when he said, "Your children need your presence more than your presents." Having a healthy relationship helps out when our kids make mistakes or we make blunders with them. Rather than the emotional intensity skyrocketing into catastrophic proportions and everyone running for offensive or defensive positions, the problem can be solved for what it is. Yes - quality relationships deliver wonderful comprehensive insurance!

A final tip

Scottish sibling researcher, Dr. Samantha Punch (2007), interviewed ninety children aged from five to seventeen years, from thirty families of mixed socioeconomic backgrounds in central Scotland. She found that kids don't have a natural incentive to treat their siblings nicely because no matter what, their sibling will still be there tomorrow! Yet, kids are more careful when it comes to how they treat their friends, because friends may not want to be their friends if they treat them unkindly.

Dr Punch's revealing conclusions included that sibling interactions tend to consist of back stage rather than front stage performances. She raised a crucial point - no matter how much we go on and on to them about treating one another well, there's simply not a lot of internal motivation for siblings to be kind and considerate to one another. As kids compete for resources, such as knowledge, attention, love, time and space, they look to parents to lead, to set the tone and cleverly tweak expectations as they grow.

Cranky kids
in the car

Ingredients:

- A car journey with kids
- A confined space with kids
- Bored kids
- Kids seeking stimulation
- Tired parents
- Parents feeling as though they should respond to every grizzle from the kids
- Parents without a plan
- A history of empty threats such as, "I'll stop the car and you can walk if you don't stop right now!"

The scenario:

When Peter meets Lydia – in the car!

It's only a fifteen minute car ride to Grandma's house, but it's on as soon as ten year old Peter and eight year old Lydia tumble into the back seat.

"Mum, Peter's keeps putting his knee on my side" calls Lydia.
"No I haven't, you are sitting over the half way line because your bum is too big," says Peter.

Mum spins around, "The car hasn't even started and we've already got an argument. It's unbelievable!"

Dad is sitting in the driver's seat shuffling through the centre console for something and doesn't want anything to do with the quarreling. He's switched off from the kids' and their backseat bickering. He wants nothing to do with it. Mum glares at him as if to say, "Thanks for nothing! Where's your support!" Dad's eyes stay intently fixed on the centre console as he searches.

You could cut the air with a knife. In the back seat Lydia and Peter continue to argue with one another in low malevolent tones. As the car starts Peter pushes his knee past the half way mark, and then quickly pulls it back before Lydia can knock it away.

Five minutes into the trip the kids are at it again.
"Lydia's got a boyfriend, Lydia's got a boyfriend, Lydia's got a boyfriend," Peter sings quietly enough to not be heard in the front seat.
Lydia, as always, takes the bait. "You're stupid, Peter. Get a life dumb boy," she shouts.
"Lydia, stop it. That's just unkind and uncalled for," grumbles mum.

Peter smirks and pushes his knee at Lydia again and Lydia slaps him on the arm. Peter deliberately overreacts with a long, loud squeal signifying the injustice.

"Cut it out you two! I'll stop this car and you can both walk the rest of the way," threatens mum.
"We are stopped... here, at the lights," Dad says sarcastically under his breath. Mum turns on him, "How is that remotely helpful Craig?"

Dad fixes his gaze on the intersection ahead and remains unhelpfully silent. He knows that Mum will be in a shocking mood towards him for the next hour and he will have to wear it.

"One more word from either of you and there'll be no dessert at Grandma's House. I'm serious, one more peep and that's it," scolds Mum.

Mum's mind wanders and she begins to daydream; "It's as if a switch is flicked as soon as they get into the car. Maybe we need a bigger car so they aren't sitting so close. Maybe we need a bus? What if we had three kids? That would be a nightmare! How would we cope then? No, that's ridiculous. Other families with cars this size have three kids in the back seat together and they cope."

Mum is suddenly jolted from her inner conversation with...
"Peter's touched me again. Stop him, mum! Do something! I hate you both for not stopping him."

"Peter - stop it," shouts Mum from the front seat.

So, how are you feeling? Has this scenario touched any memories? Are you continually dealing with complaints from the back seat? Do you have to put up with raised voices? Do you find yourself refereeing the kids' squabbles and frustrations? Does constant bickering sour trips in the car with the kids?

The annoying behaviour of kids in the car is the basis of this recipe. So often, the skittish behaviour of kids is provoked by confinement, boredom and a perfectly natural need to seek stimulation. It's how kids are wired - and occurs more so when they are confined!

Recipe rescue:

tips to make time in the car bearable, even enjoyable

If the behaviour of your children in the car drives you mad, it's time to reflect about your role in this. That's right, you've put them in the car and it's your actions and reactions that help drive their helpfulness or antagonism. Let's develop some adult thinking to encourage the behaviours we want.

Plan ahead – develop clear expectations

Prepare for the challenging situation. As you begin to buckle up and check that the kids have their seatbelts on, always state exactly what you expect from your young passengers. You might say, "Okay kids, buckle up, and remember I need you to be thoughtful passengers. I love you too much to risk driving if you're too loud or get cranky with each other."

Later, if the kids don't follow this very basic request, take a deep breath and pull the car over. Yes - pull over!

Once you have stopped, tell them about the behaviour you require. Tell them that the car is not going anywhere for three minutes while they think about changing what they're doing to something a lot more thoughtful and helpful. Don't lecture or tell off. Instead, step out of the car and remain nearby looking as relaxed as you can. Start the car when the kids agree on the right behaviour. Yes, this will probably result in delay, but in reality a few late minutes is a very minor concern. And, if you happen to be on the way to a child's birthday party, to a play over, or somewhere they have a vested interest in, then this natural consequence really delivers some clout! If the cranky backseat behaviour resumes, pull over again. You won't need to say a word, simply roll your eyes, shrug your shoulders and wait. "I'll never get anywhere on time." we hear you cry! Well, if you show the courage to do this consistently very soon your kids' cranky car behaviours will improve dramatically and there will be far, far fewer stops.

Catch the good behaviours

Bad habits sneak up on all of us, and children are even more vulnerable. At first, they tend to seek attention in negative ways because they believe it works! The golden rule is to catch the behaviours we value, and comment on them frequently. Praise is the best behaviour shaper because it alerts our kids that we are listening, participating and noticing. To catch helpful car behaviours one family decided to supply their children with a raffle ticket each time they spied one of them showing helpful car behaviour. They'd say; "Lucy, thanks for helping Juliette with her puzzle". Then, immediately, they'd hand over a raffle ticket to Lucy. The kids in this family knew that on short trips those who had 7 raffle tickets or more on the way home might be able to trade them for a treat at the shop. It wasn't fool proof, but this little investment worked wonders.

"It's my turn; I want to sit in the front with mum"

It's astounding just how long some parents choose to put up with this every time the kids head towards the car. And, it is so easily fixed! The solution - if there are two children in the family then allocate one as 'odds' and the other as 'evens'. Simply check the date, and if it's the 7th then the child who holds 'odds' has the front seat on this day. If you have more than two children then ask one of the kids to throw a dice kept in the glove compartment. Highest number takes the front seat! Alternatively ask, "who wants to be generous today and allow another to travel in the front?" This strategy can bring surprising results.

Chapter 5:
Cranky kids in the car

Pass on the responsibility

Next time one of the kids grizzles saying, "How much longer?" or "This is boring" simply agree with them! All you say is, "You're right. It's taking for ever and I'm over it as well! We should be there in half an hour." This response soothes the crankiest of kids.

Tune out

Remember, much of the quarrelling from kids in the car is for our benefit. Our response either fuels or quells it. The best approach is to stay composed. Avoid compulsively buying into the trivial. An ideal rule of thumb is to ignore two thirds of the back seat action and cautiously buy into that one third you think matters. Just think of the mum and dad in the classic 'Ultra-Tune' TV commercial!

A consequence

Consequences rarely need to be severe, just certain. The best idea is to deliver them with emotional steadiness and confidence. So when you've had enough, calmly say, "I promise a consequence to those who keep on being loud and silly. It is time to be quiet." If they fail to respond then make sure you follow through with the consequence. On arrival, you'll need to give a brief explanation as to why you are taking your child straight past their eagerly awaiting cousins or friends to a quiet room, but follow through. Your persistence will expand your children's capacity to listen, think and follow directions.

Set 'a challenge'

Set the kids a challenge! For example, you might arrange that the next two car rides without any squabbling will result in a family celebration where the kids can decide on a favourite restaurant for dinner. One bad trip doesn't reset the count back to zero; it simply means that this trip doesn't add to the tally. After the celebration dinner, the family might decide to set a goal of three 'car-free-augments' trips. With careful management, cranky car trips can become a thing of the past.

Time to talk

Many families turn car trips into opportunities to talk.

Twenty ideas to help with car trips:

1. Play Rock, Paper, Scissors,
   http://en.wikipedia.org/wiki/Rock-paper-scissors
2. Draw a letter on your child's back with a finger and see if they can guess
3. I went to the shop game,
   http://h2g2.com/dna/h2g2/A397398
4. Take off your child's shoes and socks and use them as puppets
5. Count by twos, threes, fives, tens, or count backward from 100, or teach the times tables
6. Do simple maths problems for your child to calculate mentally
7. Say words for the kids to spell
8. Play I Spy,
   http://en.wikipedia.org/wiki/I_spy
9. Play 20 Questions,
   http://en.wikipedia.org/wiki/Twenty_Questions
10. Teach your child some clapping games
    http://en.wikipedia.org/wiki/Clapping_games
11. Tell a story, taking turns one sentence at a time
12. Have your child name all his or her classmates
13. See how many people your child can name in your extended family
14. Make a Christmas or birthday wish list
15. Have a staring contest
16. Play Simon Says,
    http://en.wikipedia.org/wiki/Simon_Says
17. Play a Board game,
    http://en.wikipedia.org/wiki/Board_games
18. Play I Spy,
    http://en.wikipedia.org/wiki/I_spy
19. Play the Alphabet Game,
    http://en.wikipedia.org/wiki/Alphabet_Game
20. Play the 'Don't say NO game' where questions are asked, but NO cannot be used as an answer

Technology

Using a DS, iPad, watching a DVD or playing music on iPods or MP3 players, on long car trips helps keep kids entertained.

Follow the map

Go to 'Google Maps' and print a series of strip maps showing the journey. Give a set to each child with a marker and see if they can find roads, creeks, rivers, towns, parks, playgrounds, lookouts, forests, state borders, main road intersections, and colour or circle them. Every so often, tell them something that is coming up soon and see who's able to spot it first.

When all else fails on long trips

When the kids become restless and relentless, the best thing to do is pull over for a while at a school playground, a MacDonald's or a playing field. Let your kids play for half an hour. You might keep them moving by using a frisbee, skipping rope, netball or football, and when they have burnt their surplus energy continue on.

Ingredients:

- A child or teen who wants control
- A parent who wants control
- An audience of onlookers
- A frazzled parent
- A tired, hungry or overstimulated kid
- A child who believes throwing a tantrum gets results!
- A parent with a history of giving in to tantrums
- A parent still learning how-to reward positive behaviour and disengage from negative behaviour

Recipe rescue:

designs to phase-out tantruming behaviours in children and young teens

The scenarios...

Knowing it is different to doing it

"When my five year old Talia gets upset because she's heard "no" or doesn't get her way she spins right out of control, and its fast! There's always screaming and telling us off, and anybody who tries to intervene gets punched, kicked or smacked. At this moment, there's nothing I can do to calm her down.

I know I shouldn't give in to her. I know the theory about what I should do and at home I tend to do it, mostly. However, when she tantrums in public I feel judged by onlookers. That rocks my confidence and I turn to jelly. I know they just want me to shut her up. That's when all the theory goes out the window. I simply don't have the time or the courage to do what I know I should."

At the supermarket

Five year old Timmy begins tugging at Mummy's shirt while they are at the supermarket checkout. Timmy has spotted the Kinder Surprises. Well, they weren't hard to miss - conveniently shelved at his eye level.

"Timmy, you can't have one. Please don't do that"
"Timmy, that makes me sad when you do that. Now be a good boy and leave Mummy's shirt alone"
"Darling, you can see I'm busy with the lady"
"Timmy, be a good boy and do what I ask?"
"Timmy, let go please"
"Timmy, stop that please"
"Timmy, stop it!"
"Timmy, stop that now, please?"
"Timmy, if you do what Mummy says there's a chocolate frog in my bag for you"
"Timmy, leave my bag alone. Mummy will get the chocolate frog out for you later.

"Timmy, be a good boy. Don't make me sad"
"Timmy, put Mummy's bag down please"
"Timmy, come back with the bag"
"Timmy, we don't hit, do we?"
"Timmy, if you hit Mummy again, there won't be a frog"
"Timmy, if you hit Mummy again, there won't be a frog"
"Timmy, if you hit Mummy again, there won't be a frog"
"Once more Timmy, no frog, remember"
"Timmy. That really hurt Mummy. Did you want to hurt Mummy? Do you want to make mummy sad?"

Mum and Timmy get through the checkout and Timmy finally throws a tantrum next to the service counter.

Mum hurriedly gives him the chocolate frog from her bag to quieten him down, but that's not enough, Timmy is entranced by the Kinder Surprise. The tantrum escalates as Timmy throws the chocolate across the floor. "Oh for goodness sake, I'll buy the Kinder if you just be quiet!"

Tantrums are dirty bombs!

The word 'tantrum' strikes dread into the hearts of most parents. Some carry memories etched into their minds, some are still experiencing their children's tantrums and a few unlucky ones have young teens who've not grown through them and now produce expert performances. It seems no place is safe when it comes to throwing a temper tantrum - the supermarket, kiss and drop at school, birthday parties, the bank, at home, with relatives or friends - anywhere. In fact, it seems that the more we're on guard for 'tanty-styled behaviours', the higher the likelihood of one of our kids throwing it. Just as sharks smell blood, kids and young teens seem to smell that we're on edge or our resources are depleted, and it's time to pounce!

Many tantrums are designed to happen in front of an audience - this adds all the more clout to control parents. Other temper explosions just happen in the moment, but one thing is certain, tantrums are dirty bombs. They're ugly and loud, and sometimes there's the added bonus of tears, snot and expletives! Tantrums send emotional shockwaves that triggers distress in all human beings within earshot. In such moments, our brain cells scramble and find it hard to connect with one another. The idea of making a sensible decision about how-to stick to the plan we decided on earlier fades fast.

Let's begin by looking at a few FACTS about tantrums. By the way, our advice applies to all children - 3 to 14 years.

Fact one:

Step back from the noise, the irritation and the embarrassment. Accept that temper tantrums are a normal part of a child's behaviour. The tantrum is a horribly misguided way for kids to take control of situations as they nudge towards making more independent decisions. It's all very healthy stuff! Most kids will give tantrums a 'red-hot-go' between eighteen months and four years of age. If a child learns early that their tantrum gets them what they want, a seed is planted and they'll use them more often, and well past the classic tantrum ages.

Fact two:

Tantrums come in all sorts of flavours - they are very much a part of a child's personality. Think about your child's personal qualities. Is your child strong willed, knows their mind, a perfectionist, anticipates how things should work out, proud, stubborn, intelligent, sensitive or independent? These are wonderful human qualities. However, in kids who will not or cannot self-regulate, these qualities jump to full-throttled, angry explosions. Personality plays a big role in how tantrums look and how long they last. In younger kids, tantrums can be angry explosions where they completely lose it. Some involve screaming, crying, tensing the body, stiffening of limbs, throwing the head about and flailing arms, resembling the moves of a break dancer. In extreme cases, kids will break things or find somebody to hurt in order to achieve indiscriminate revenge. A few upset themselves to the point of vomiting or holding their breath until their colour changes!

Fact three:

A tantrum usually involves at least one, or all, of these ingredients - disappointment, tiredness, stress, hunger or overstimulation.

Fact four:

When a kid explodes, it may not be a sign of disobedience or defiance. For some kids, overstimulation comes all too easily because their sensory system hits overdrive all too fast. This is often the case for children who are on Autism spectrum. The tantrum is their body's immediate defence response against a loud or frightening environment. Their senses are literally being assaulted! Similarly, a tantrum styled eruption may indicate intense emotional overload by a child who is usually mild mannered, but cannot process or intellectualise an appropriate course of action just at that moment. Where a computer will freeze when it has too much input, some kids will tantrum. With this in mind, try not to jump to conclusions the next time you see a parent dealing with their child's tantrum. There may well be deep-seated, invisible reasons at play.

Fact five:

The supermarket, shops and the shopping mall are not your friends. Marketing researchers confirm what most of us intuitively know. Many of the kids who tantrum in these situations are actually set up by clever shop psychology to do so. These vendors know how and what appeals to kids - a tin of Barbie spaghetti shapes, a box of cereal with a kid's movie character smirking at them, or sweets and soft drinks strategically placed at the checkout. Make no mistake, advertisers and retailers are frighteningly efficient at finding the triggers to make kids want. A larger percentage of their sales than you might imagine are reliant on parents giving in to demanding children.

Fact six:

A few older children and young teens continue to tantrum to get their way. While there are many varied and complex reasons for this, it is often linked to the fact they believe tantruming will get them what they want. Here's a compelling reason to start early to fine-tune your response, even if it challenges what feels 'natural' to you. It is a fact - teenage tantrums evolve into something far trickier to deal with than those of young children. Their tantrums are usually sophisticated, calculated and sustained, and can leave families deeply distressed and in hardship. We have seen teen tantrums specialising in threats, theft, credit card fraud, running away from home, forgery, lying, violence, publicly humiliating parents and so on and so on - all in order to get their way and have their immediate 'wants' met. Outside of the family in real life, such actions towards others would be regarded with a criminal intent.

Recipe rescue:

designs to phase-out tantruming behaviours in children and young teens

So, what's a parent to do when their little darling, or not so little darling, turns into a raging bull? This Recipe rescue explores a few very practical ideas to handle these tricky behaviours.

Golden Rules:

☒ Never respond to your child's tantrum with your own brand of 'bad' behaviour

☒ Do not give into tantrums, otherwise you reward your child's anti-social behaviour

☑ Learn how-to behave in tantrum moments so you don't strengthen them and associated negative behaviours.

☑ In time, because of the cool, calm way you react, your child will learn that this is not an effective way to get what they want

Timing is everything!

Sometimes kids get locked into phases where they tantrum, and all your talking, bribing and threatening doesn't seem to make a bit of difference. If you're facing this, a good approach is to stop bringing them to the shops or the supermarket for a while in order to break the cycle. Later, when you begin taking them again, be sure to get the timing right. At the end of the day, just before dinner is a recipe for 'the perfect storm'- they're hungry, tired, worn out and restless, even before you walk in the doors! Plan ahead and consider when the kids are likely to have optimal tolerance.

Chapter 6:
Tantrums

Triggers and distraction

All behaviours have triggers. Kids are generally triggered into tantrums because they want something, have been told 'no', or have been asked to do something. Most outbursts take place in vibrant, stimulating, public situations because there's so much on offer and so much at stake. If you're not sure about their triggers, then start to gather a little data so you're able to build a clearer picture. Keep some notes about where and when tantrums take place and look for patterns. This is invaluable information.

Once you have their triggers broadly worked out, think creatively to find ideas to 'circuit break' those flashpoints. For littlies; take a muesli bar from your bag and give it to your child as you reach the supermarket checkout, have 20 cents ready for them to put it in the plastic charity dog once through the checkout. For not so littlies; get them to tally the shopping bill as you go and if they're within $5 of the final amount give them a small prize! Get them to push the trolley or drag along their own trolley, or give them a small supplementary shopping list and let them track down the items and meet you back at the checkout.

Clever parents become masters of distraction and continue to tweak what they do to match the maturity of their children. They realise that distraction effectively bumps kids of all ages away from the road to 'tanty-town'. Keep a few essentials in your bag that can be pulled out when you sense the storm approaching - something to eat or play with can quickly short circuit tantrums.

Plan ahead - be upfront and call it!

If you anticipate a tantrum over the small packet of Mentos, perfectly positioned at four year old eye level at the checkout, why not tell your child that they can have the packet? The deal is if they are helpful during shopping - give them something to do - their reward will be the Mentos! If their behaviour becomes ugly or they tantrum, endure the storm but do not give them the Mentos.

Say what you mean

"Last call. We're leaving in three minutes"
"The Xbox has to be off at ten o'clock"
"In five minutes it will be time to get out of the pool"
"One more turn and then its hop off time"
"One more ad break, then it's time for bed"

As soon as these words fly out of your mouth, they actually become a living contract with your kids. If you break this contract, you have broken a promise. This is serious! If your kids are used to you saying "in five minutes" and it really means "in twenty minutes", or later, of course they will argue the point or tantrum when you finally get round to expecting their cooperation. To understand the frustration they feel from your unpredictability, just imagine how you would feel if you had

a boss that constantly let you miss work deadlines and one day, sacked you for not meeting one deadline. You'd feel like throwing a tantrum too.

Be confident and authoritative

When your child starts to complain; "how much longer", "why can't I have it?", "we've been here for ages", "I'm bored", or wants something you're not prepared to give, do not go defensive!

 EXAMPLES of DEFENSIVE one-liners from parents

"Not much longer. Please, please be good for mummy"
"I know darling. Sorry! Can we stay just five minutes longer?"
"We've only been here five minutes. I'm going as fast as I can"
"You were the one that said you wanted to come. Now you're upsetting me"
"We've only been here an hour - how much longer can you last? You tell me?"
"When I was a kid I had to …"
"You kids are so spoiled …"

 EXAMPLES of CONFIDENT and AUTHORITATIVE one-liners from parents

"Yeah, me too. I'm tired of being here as well"
"I'm over it too – thanks for hanging in there!"
"It's a pain when you can't have something you want isn't it?"
"I get how you feel - I'd love a new car!"
"Buck up. Not much I can do, but time goes faster when you put yourself in a happier mood"
"I agree. It's disappointing when the fun has to end. That's the way it is"

Statements delivered in an authoritative tone are more likely to settle the frayed emotions of kids or a child looking for a fight. When we choose to go on attack, or offer sooky defensive statements, we're more likely to trigger poor or hostile behaviour in our children.

winning recipe - "don't look at them, don't talk to them and don't let them win" - but this takes poise and self-control on your part. The skills you've developed around 'tactically ignoring' misbehaviour will come in very handy here (to recap on tactical ignoring see the chapter, How-to catch and build positive behaviours).

How do you manage not to look at them and not to talk to them while they're tantruming? Distance will help. There are two types of 'distance' parents can use to communicate that they won't be part of a child's negative behaviour. One is emotional distance and the other is physical distance.

Being clear reduces misunderstandings and tantrums

As you leave home make it crystal clear to the kids what will be happening. For instance;
"Kids, we are dropping over to Josh's house to return his bathers. We won't go inside - it's not a play over because we are due at Nanna and Pop's in fifteen minutes".
Every time you do this, you minimise the chance of nasty disappointments arising. Kids who know what will happen naturally feel more settled and better able to cope. It's worth mentioning here, that if you were invited into Josh's house while dropping off his bathers, you'd need to politely decline and explain that you cannot stay. You made a contract with the kids - it's a promise worth keeping for all sorts of reasons!

Check your paranoia!

When a child is tantruming at full-throttle it's hard for anyone to turn a blind eye. Who could ignore such an energetic and compelling force of nature? The added attraction, of course, is that most passing by have been in a similar situation themselves. Their odd looks mightn't be unkind, judgemental or disapproving. The smirk on their face and downcast eyes likely has more to do with them recalling an incident that they've faced, and a sense of relief that it's you dealing with it this time. And, for those few who shoot an obvious

disapproving look, well, you can survive without their approval. They don't matter.

There's a flip side to this as well. The next time you're near someone with a tantruming child, make a sympathetic comment to them; "Hang in there, it will pass", "Tough stuff. Better you than me", "It's such hard work. May the force be with you", or "I dealt with one of these last week. It's exhausting!"

Kind words are always appreciated, even if a stressed parent takes a few moments to process what you said to them.

"Don't look at them, don't talk to them and don't let them win"

If there's ever a time to develop a steely resolve and a planned approach as a parent, it has to be in the moment when your child is tantruming. During this, you'll need to gather all of your grit to help your child over this ugly hump. The worst thing you can do is to give in to their demands. This will encourage them to continue temper tantrums every time they want something, or when something goes wrong. The

Emotional distance

This is created as you switch your attention away from your child to something else. You might turn away and check your phone for messages, have a drink, or gaze at an interesting person in the distance - your look and your body language literally imagines that the tantrum has no impact on you whatsoever. If you are in a place where a tantrum can go on without seriously affecting others, most onlookers will quickly work out that you are tactically ignoring your child. And who knows, you might end up in an engaging conversation with a sympathetic onlooker that really switches your attention right away from the tantrum!

Physical distance

This is created as you physically move away from your child. Move far enough so you are clear of the emotional vortex they are busy generating. Keep yourself safe from flying emotional shrapnel. This should help you to keep your poise and your resolve. The tantrum will pass.

The worst thing you can do is to give in to their demands. This will encourage them to continue temper tantrums every time they want something, or when something goes wrong

Take them out!

No, not in the gangland sense! Suppose the tantrum takes place somewhere you cannot ignore it? What if it happens in church, or during a concert where others are a captive audience to your child's tantrum and it will badly affect their experience? The not-so-easy answer is to remove the child from the environment - take them out!

This is where many parents go wobbly at the knees. They know that moving towards their child, picking them up and removing them will result in ear-splitting screaming and shameless protests. Naturally, they feel uncomfortable about being 'the spectacle' as their child squirms and struggles with them. There is no doubt that this will be a less-than-graceful exit and is likely to replace the main event, well, just for a moment! This is the point where a few parents decide it's easier to give in to their child or ignore their anti-social behaviour. This is not a good way to go, because fairness to others must

always be considered. It's just not fair to keep a tantruming child in a space like this. This is the time to take charge. Trust us, your decisive leadership in this moment will be appreciated by every onlooker. You will earn their sympathy and respect, and instantly the audience will think, "I'm glad that parent took that poor child out". They will understand.

Once removed, your child is likely to continue their tantrum for a while. As it subsides, let them know that having a tantrum was a poor choice. Reassure them that you're pleased the 'silly' tantrum has gone keep it very brief. A lecture or a telling off won't help at this point.

A consequence always follows a tantrum

Let your children know in advance, in happier times, that a tantrum will always result in a consequence. The consequence doesn't have to be delivered or even mentioned while your child's tantrum is in full swing. It can be applied later, at home. Your child does not choose the consequence, you do. And, once you announce it another tantrum may be set off, and when this happens, our advice is to ignore this next tantrum and follow through with the one consequence that you have chosen. Simple negative consequences include; the loss of a privilege, missing out on the next scheduled visit to where the tantrum happened (if it was a place the child wanted to be), missing out on something expected,

time alone, early to bed and so on. Negative consequences should never be vengeful. They are used to get the message across that the child's behaviour was unacceptable and they are capable of making much better choices.

On the flip side, remember the theme of the chapter, How-to catch and build positive behaviours. In this chapter we share the art of how-to positively influence the behaviour of children by orchestrating situations to catch them doing the behaviours we value. Giving attention to kids in this way is like fertilising the behaviours we want to see more of.

Catch the tantrum early - give your child choice

As you see the early warning signs building, move close to your child, gently meet their gaze and quietly help them check their behaviour;

> "I can see you're thinking about a tantrum. You don't have to, we can talk."
>
> "It's your choice; you can tantrum or you can make a better choice."
>
> "If you tantrum here, there will be a consequence when you get home."
>
> "You choose; you can have a tantrum or have an ice-cream after we've finished."

Try giving them a choice rather than becoming demanding or trying to intimidate them into submissiveness. Giving permission to choose will give some kids permission to jump tracks and respond in refreshing ways. The element of surprise can deliver stunning results!

Let your children know in advance, in happier times, that a tantrum will always result in a consequence.

How might have mummy handled Timmy differently?

Isn't hindsight infuriating? But let's use it anyway. Go back to the beginning of the chapter and quickly review the scenario, 'At the supermarket'. This is where five year old Timmy started tugging at his mother's shirt while they were closing in on the supermarket checkout.

In the space of a minute or two, Mummy used about 180 words to reason with Timmy. Yet Timmy's behaviour went from bad to worse. Mummy felt flustered and Timmy won the Kinder Surprise. Why?

Well, mummy wasn't up for the challenge. A tired child, her inexperience with handling tantrums well and the cleverly placed chocolate were too strong a combination. Mummy tried to appeal to Timmy's better nature. Alas at four years of age, and in this kind of moment, Timmy isn't developmentally ready for this wordy, moral style of parenting. Timmy had only one goal – to get the Kinder Surprise!

Timmy is a normal little boy who spun out of control because he was tired, hungry and influenced by shrewd shop psychology. He needed decisive leadership from his mum, but didn't get it. Mummy failed to tell Timmy what she wanted him to do - she failed to promise him a consequence after asking him twice to be a "good boy", and rewarded his meltdown with the frog that was initially offered for cooperative behaviour. How utterly confusing for Timmy! The consequence of this is that next time at the checkout, we're likely see the very same performance by Timmy - not what mummy wants at all!

TIMMY's and Mum's replay

Mummy and Timmy enter the checkout.

Before Timmy starts to ramp up his complaining, Mummy says, "We're almost finished Timmy. When we are done, there's a chocolate frog in my bag for you for being so patient"

Timmy spots the Kinder Surprise. He grabs Mummy's shirt, and directs her to look at it.

"Timmy… I'm not buying that today. Let go."
"Timmy, if you pull my shirt again you won't get the chocolate frog. You won't get anything. Use your patience"

Timmy's Mum has a history of following through with promises. Timmy begins to surrender and Mummy provides appropriate feedback, "That's great Timmy. It helps when you are patient"

After 10 seconds Timmy pulls Mummy's shirt again and groans longingly as he looks at the Kinder Surprise.

"Timmy… you just pulled my shirt again. That's a shame. We'll have to keep the chocolate frog for next time"

Timmy cries loudly. Mummy ignores. Many eyes are on her, but hers stay fixed on the groceries as the checkout attendant scans items and bundles them into bags. She's well aware of Timmy's loud sobs, but determined to give no attention to them. After 30 seconds of ignoring mummy turns to Timmy and firmly says…

"That's enough Timmy, you can stop crying now"
"Okay, let's get some lunch"

Timmy asks if he can have the chocolate frog with lunch.

"No Timmy, you pulled my shirt after I asked you not to. That was a bad choice. Never mind. I'll keep the treat safe for another time".

With fewer words, a firm promise and decisive follow through, Timmy begins to see that Mummy is a woman of her word. He gets a sense that she's trustworthy, in charge and is leading. Next time at the supermarket checkout, Timmy is far more likely to listen to his Mum.

Chapter 7:

Dressing dilemmas

Recipe rescue:

tips to extinguish dramatic dressing dilemmas

Ingredients:

- A child who needs to be 'the boss'
- A child who knows how-to grab attention
- A child who's learnt how-to inconvenience others to get noticed
- Parents who don't know how-to deal with their child's grab for power
- A wardrobe with too many choices
- A child exposed to too many dressing influences - television, internet, friends and flashy role models
- Parents who've unwittingly bought into the drama by allowing multiple clothes changes in the past
- Busy lives, busy mornings and time-tight schedules

The scenarios...

Is it a body image issue or a play for power?

It's starting younger with kids nowadays! Is it genetic? How on earth can a four year old be having body-image issues and a styling crisis? Lately we have three changes of clothes and a tantrum before we go out. Some mornings I can't get anything on her and we end up being late. Once I finally do get something on her she stands in front of her mirror and screams, "I hate my clothes and this looks ugly!

They're my clothes and I'll wear them how I like!

It's ridiculous. He wants to wear shorts and a t-shirt in the middle of winter. I can't let him out of the house dressed like that! He's six. Surely he knows better! What will people think of my parenting when he stands there shivering in the supermarket car park?

Is the frightful scene the reward this child is pushing for?

My ten year old daughter doesn't want to wear any clothes we put out for her and she's got plenty. She'd rather go through the washing basket and take out the dirty clothes she wore yesterday. Bottom line is that she won't put on anything I suggest without a frightful scene.

"But, darling, you look beautiful"

It came to a head last night when we were getting ready for a family party at the kids' Grandparents' house. My wife and my daughter, eleven year old Francesca, had agreed the night before about what she was going to wear. I ironed the outfit for Francesca. The next day, as we were all getting ready Francesca started crying saying she didn't want to wear what was decided. My wife proceeded to iron four outfits, which were all rejected with ever increasing amounts of crying. In the end Francesca threw a full blown tantrum. I tried to calm her down, and give her another option. She grabbed a top that was lying behind her door on the floor. It was dirty and had a small hole in it. I told her that the top wasn't an option. Another tantrum followed. Then she wanted to put on an old pair of trainers which I told her were for around home. This was followed by "nobody cares about how I want to look". Heartbroken, I told her that she looked beautiful in the outfit we first decided on. We spent another half an hour arguing, and the more we tried to help the more she fought us. By this time I was done! So I said, "Right, okay, I'll call Grandma and Grandpa and tell them we're not coming now."

Why so much drama?

For some parents, getting the right clothes on children in the time available is a high stress moment. When time is tight and there's a lot to do, the dressing dilemmas seem to intensify. Yet, beginning to have a say in what to wear is a 'big kid' thing to do and it brings kids a sense of identity, pride and satisfaction. In many families however, what starts out as a much celebrated rite of passage quickly turns sour as the child becomes overawed by too many variables. The demands of rushed mornings, having to conform to adult expectations and processing the dressing stereotypes provided from television and peer groups make choices all the more complicated!

Quite often there's an additional event at play as well! For kids who have a natural desire to be in control, the drama over getting dressed puts them at centre stage. It guarantees that most mornings, or during those final moments as the family is due to rush out the door everything becomes focused on them. In this case, it's not only about what shirt to wear, but it's about the unconscious satisfaction that comes from keeping their stressed-out parents really busy with them. We've all experienced it - the shouting, pleading, bargaining and threatening as we desperately offer a smorgasbord of pants, shirts, socks and jumpers trying to appease an upset child. Notice that we did say unconscious satisfaction. Before you dismiss this notion by saying, "Oh, my child is way too distressed during these moments to enjoy the power". Believe us, the emotional vortex that these moments create actually scratches an unconscious itch for drama in some kids regardless of how upset they get.

Recipe rescue:

tips to extinguish dramatic dressing dilemmas

If the scenarios above resonate with what's happening in your home, then the vital ingredient to turn it around is to review your thinking and your response. If you really want to steady the emotional tone over dressing dilemmas, we're asking you to be courageous and look at the fundamental ingredients at play. We know that we're likely to lose a few of you here - those parents who secretly enjoy the drama, and love telling their 'facebook friends' how hard it is to get their kids dressed in the morning, those parents who must remain a part of the conflict in order to feel good about their mothering or fathering, and those parents who brag about the very special martyrdom such battles bestow on them! These are parents who are entrenched in the 'permissive' or 'neglectful' social control windows (to recap see the Introduction).

> *If you really want to steady the emotional tone over dressing dilemmas we're asking you to be courageous and look at the fundamental ingredients at play.*

For those of you who have a resolve to make positive changes to the dressing dilemmas, stick with us, you won't be disappointed.

Practice and preparation

As you adopt this new approach actually explain how the arrangement is to work to each of your children. When you sort through their wardrobe invite them to help you cull their clothes. Decide together which clothes must go to charity, to family and friends, or are to be packed away for posterity. A wonderful way to save tears is to pack clothes that have reached their 'used by date', but remain special, away safely and securely for your children to keep!

Remember, this is not an exercise in winning their approval for the new system. Parenting effectively is not a popularity contest. More to the point, this is an exercise to show your clever leadership, so as the parent, you have the final say. The way to work it is to let your child know what will be happening and what they can expect from now on. Consequently, don't ask questions as, "Is that alright?" or "Do you like this idea?" or "Do you think we can make this work?" If you do, you won't like the responses you get from any of your kids!

Choice

Firstly, human beings don't do choice very well. Too much choice is confusing, especially when you are young and your brain is still a long, long way from being fully developed. It's a well recognised fact that if you put too many choices in front of someone, they will be less likely to make a choice than if the choices were limited. Just look at supermarket psychology - they know this, and deliberately limit your choice of brands of jam, for instance, because they know you'll leave with no jam if you are overwhelmed by too many brand choices.

Use this very same principle with young children and their wardrobe. Regularly cull clothes from their wardrobes and drawers - it reduces clutter, confusion and unnecessary choices. In winter, pack away the 'summer-only' clothes or put them out of sight where they can't be grabbed. Some of our clever parents adopt the strategy of only presenting occasion-suitable clothes for their kids to dress into. Others put out just two outfits for their youngsters to choose from. When a child rejects both choices, the deal is that the parent chooses. Then, they calmly leave the outfit for the child to dress in. When you begin this, make a bargain with yourself to not react to the grizzles that will inevitably come as you do this. A good leader is

able to stay firm and unflappable. Your child's flare-up is their attempt to draw you back into to a dressing dilemma.

Resistance is normal

Now, here's the critical part of this Recipe rescue. If things are currently challenging at dressing time, then expect resistance to the approach outlined just above. If the drama has more to do with taking control than it has to do with what to wear, they won't give this power up gladly. Who can blame them? Having control and exercising power over a family is intoxicating for some kids, and when they've become accustomed to running the show they will not surrender easily. So, be prepared - their battle for control may move to the breakfast table, or to the bathroom, or to what will or will not go into their lunchbox for school. Our advice - be that good leader and remain firm and unflappable. Your child's eruption is their attempt to draw you back into the fight.

Dressing without television

Have you noticed the type of advertising that bombards kids on TV in the mornings and afternoons? The wrong advert at the wrong time can easily prompt a desire for a change in the selection of clothes for a child who may be feeling a bit wobbly about their image. Just like the junk food companies, those who create kid's clothes know the best times to screen their calculating commercials. Taking TV out of the picture during dressing time is one less troublesome influence in more ways than one. Just getting side tracked from getting dressed by what's on TV can be trouble in itself.

A good leader is able to stay firm and unflappable. Your child's flare-up is their attempt to draw you back into to a dressing dilemma.

Spare clothes in the car

In the right moment, when you're feeling relaxed and the kids are in a receptive mood, explain that the consequence for not getting dressed on any school morning will be that they'll leave the house in whatever they wore to bed. Have ready a 'generic-styled' outfit that lives in the car for them to slide into, but don't make it something they'll want to wear - just a slightly more respectable option than pyjamas! A similar plan, used determinedly, can work a treat at other times as well. Just pop them in the car in their 'around home' clothes and let them decide on route whether they stay in these clothes or change into the clothes you have selected for them. It's amazing how quickly a young overwhelmed human being can calm down and recover when the choices they have are made clear to them.

Vulnerable emerging identity

Is a negative perception about their body image created more often in kids whose parents constantly fight with them over dressing? Commonsense and a smattering of research tell us that this is likely the case. This is why we recommend clear and consistent leadership from parents - try to stay steady and composed even when under pressure. Just glance back at the beginning of the chapter when eleven year old Francesca was dressing for a family party. Her Father's approach of trying to soothe her by going through a series of outfit changes was a poor choice, despite the fact he was well intentioned. The golden rule - getting too involved, over-talking and trying to sympathise unwittingly sends the message, "Oh yes, it is very, very important how you look, and without the perfect look and outfit, you're not okay." And, it got worse because in his distress, he told her that "she looked beautiful in the outfit first decided on." It could have been easily misconstrued by Francesca that she looked beautiful because of the outfit!

As we mention throughout the book - it's wise to persistently review what we say and do in all matters with our kids.
So next time, when you're faced with a dressing dilemma, ponder these questions;

Does my child imitate the way I go on as I get dressed for an event?

Do I need to be modelling more apt behaviours as I ready myself for an occasion?

Am I too openly critical about dress sense, labels and the appearance of others in front of my children?

Are my kids doing much the same?

Am I too vain about my public appearance and consequently too severe on my kids?

Do I give my kids opportunities to express themselves through the clothes they choose to wear?

When my child chooses to wear something not quite appropriate, should I consider a different tack and say, "I know you love those clothes, but they're too good for a 'play over'. I'd really like you to wear these, but you can choose this time"?

Is their dramatic dressing dilemma more about them exercising control? If it is, then what's the best way to handle an obstinate child? (for helpful information see the chapters, How-to catch and build positive behaviours and The 'art' of managing tricky kid behaviour)

Will my response deliver the message I want them to receive?

What is the message I want them to hear?

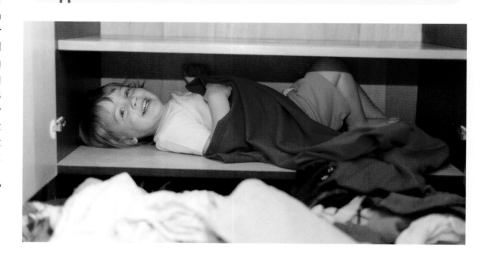

Chapter 8:

"Get off that computer, now!"

Recipe rescue:

savvy ideas to balance the use of big and small screens

The scenario...

"Get off that computer, now!"

"Joel, for the fifth and final time get off that computer, now!" pleads his mother.

Eleven year old Joel soothes Aimee by calling out, "still saving it mum. It's just taking a long time."
"It always takes a long time. Just goes to show how much better we'd all be if you took up reading or magic tricks. Hurry up! You've got homework to do," calls Aimee.
"Mum I think the computer might have a virus. Could be why it's running slow. I'll do a check while it saves my game," Joel calls.
"Thank you, but that's not really helping me. I need you off the computer to do your homework. It's getting late."

Aimee decides to investigate. Joel doesn't hear her approaching his bedroom. Joel is startled and minimises his game screen to hide what he's up to. It's too late! Aimee caught sight of the game as Joel reduced it to the toolbar.

"Joel you're such a liar. You had no intention of getting off the computer. You're making up all kinds of stupid excuses to stay on it," Aimee screams as she pulls the power cord from the wall.

The screen crackles into blankness. Joel watches his mother take the power cord and keyboard and storm out of his room. He follows her with his iPad in hand.
"What do you think you're doing with that? How dare you! You've got homework to do," barks Aimee.

"This is my school iPad. My homework is on it," says Joel apologetically. Aimee supervises Joel closely while he completes his homework. She's fuming, and once he's finished, she snatches the iPad from him for safe keeping.

"Joel, I'm fed up with your lies. You'll say anything to have more and more time on the computer. You're addicted. Let's see how you go over the next week without any screens whatsoever!" announces Aimee.
"I'm sorry mum. I'll go and have a shower and get to bed," Joel quietly responds.

An hour later, in the darkness of his bedroom and under the bedcovers, Joel isn't drifting off to sleep. He's on high alert playing his new game on Nintendo DSi.

Finding a balance takes more than you think!

The intoxicating appeal of video games is understandable - they're fun, the action is fast and furious, the challenges are inviting, and screens have the capacity to feed the brain with rich visual and auditory stimuli. This stimulus is so powerful that while engaged, our brains set up a tantalizing positive feedback loop hard to tear away from. Given that the 'off switches' in kids' brains aren't fully developed until they reach their mid to late twenties, it's no wonder so many find it hard to self-regulate. Even the basic act of receiving a text message triggers the brain's reward centre! It's like a hit from a drug and the more you get and send, the better you feel. What about you? Can you resist the siren call from a status update from 'facebook'?

Each of us have to deal with a backdrop of extremist chatter, warning that kids are fast becoming video game addicted, internet obsessed and that a cyberspace predator is just a click away. These devotees will shout from the roof tops that studies link excessive screen-time with depression, sleep, anxiety, posture problems, back pain and issues concerning kid's attention spans, socialisation and obesity, let alone their risk of exposure to inappropriate pictures, video and information. They'll trot out facts we've long known about with their chilling spin on it. They'll quote a latest piece of research to prove that those who constantly use computers and mobile phones are more likely to develop stress symptoms, depression and two heads. They'll also tell you that internet overuse, obsessive computer use and problematic overexposure to screens has become so bad that it will be added to the Diagnostic and Statistical Manual of Mental Disorders (DSM-V) and be called 'Internet Addiction Disorder' (IAD).

While IAD looks set to be added to the DSM-V, clinicians are already offering expensive digital detox programs for so called addicted kids and adults! No one in their right mind would deny that pathological screen use severely restricts living a balanced life. It's just plain common sense - 'moderation in all things' or you risk living with dysfunction. We are not alarmists and reject hysterical calls suggesting that all kids are becoming addicted to screens. Instead, we'd like to take you down a road where your poise, leadership and ingenuity creates an approach to help kids find balance between screens and other aspects of living a real life. Working towards a balance is a much healthier approach than coming down heavily on kids by banning, hiding and blatantly limiting screens and devices. Heavy handedness is more likely to push kids into becoming oppositional and deceitful.

Recipe rescue:

savvy ideas to balance the use of big and small screens

Let's be real. Most kids, and quite a few adults, have trouble turning off screens.

> *In this chapter the term 'screens' include big and small screens; computers, iPads, iPods, Surfaces, Xbox's, handheld PlayStations, smartphones, DS's, televisions and so on. This list will be obsolete in five years, but you get the idea!*

The goal of this Recipe rescue is to develop approaches to skilfully support kids to find balance between time on screens and other activities. The foundation has got be a trusting relationship, because as your kids mature, you won't be able to monitor everything they do. Good screen habits and routines are best established early on and embedded in 'good sense' rather than being seen by kids as a rule to break.

You will not like this Recipe rescue if you have frequently used screens to babysit your children. If you have, and you can't see this, then forget what follows. Your dependency on having the babysitter will outweigh any intelligent suggestion we might offer. Similarly, you will not like this Recipe rescue if you are a screen addict yourself and won't change.

Chapter 8:

"Get off that computer, now!"

What's happening at home at the moment? Here are a few questions to help you put things into perspective;

— Is your child's drive to be attached to screens getting in the way of living a well-balanced life shared between friends, relaxation, school, study, sport, family interactions, play and exercise?

— Is your child fanatical about getting to a screen each day?

— Does your child believe that access to a screen each day is their 'God-given' right?

— Is your child stuck to the keyboard or controller for hours on end?

— Do you see an increase in hostile thinking and the acting out of more aggressive behaviours following your child's stint with video games?

— Are you noticing that they tend to drill everyone about their latest video game, and it seems to consume conversations?

— Does their devotion to screens - getting on and off of them - often cause upsets within the family?

If you've answered "yes" to just a few of these questions then you know that now is the time to introduce a little more balance in the use of big and small screens. Let's begin.

How much is too much time in front of screens?

In May, 2012, Dr Aric Sigman condensed an array of research about the impact of excessive screen-time on the physical and mental health of children and teens. He told the Royal College of Paediatrics' annual conference that;

- *Littlies under 3 years of age should have little or no screen time*
- *Children from 4 to 8 years should not exceed 90 minutes per day*
- *Teens under 18 years should have a maximum of 2 hours a day*

His proposal falls into line with the recommendations of most child development experts.

We respect that parents have a right to choose how carefully they apply and stick with such guidelines. Our question is, "Why would a parent choose to ignore them when the evidence concerning children's wellbeing and excessive screen-time continues to build into a disquieting picture?"

Observe and record

To work out whether your kids are spending too much time on screens, start charting or logging the time they spend on them. After doing this ever so inconspicuously for a fortnight, study your results and compare their on screen-time to the recommended guidelines. Also, take notice of what your child is playing on screens. Affectionately introduce the term 'screen rubbish', which describe games that are all about fast trigger and mindless amusement! There's nothing wrong with a little 'screen rubbish' in everyone's diet, as it can be quite therapeutic!

If you think screen-time is excessive and you decide to act on it, we suggest that a collaborative approach is the first tool of choice. Talk to the kids about their unbalanced screen usage. If they are older, share the research with them. Show them just how much time they're clocking up and what's recommended. Explain that it's not your intention to take the screens away because you know how much enjoyment they get from them. Appeal to their trust in you to bring better balance into their lives. As you know, old habits die hard.

A compassionate word

Some children, especially those on the Autism spectrum become fixated on screens and video games very easily. Their appetite for these is insatiable, and excessiveness is rampant. Tread gently here, but it is imperative to gradually bring balance into their lives as well. While they may use screens to wind down and regroup emotionally, it is important that they actually earn extra screen-time by being cooperative, helpful and agreeable. Some of these kids are so lonely that the computer has gradually become a substitute for face to face social contact and amusement. Take it gently as you re-establish a balance, but a better balance must be the end goal here.

Enlightenment isn't being a 'screen Nazi'?

Do you act and sound like a 'screen Nazi'? Do you swing between permissive and punitive, one day allowing them to spend hours of uninterrupted screen time and then the next day deciding they are screen addicts and you must ban screens? Instead of gently developing proactive plans around the sensible use of screens, do you find yourself screeching, "For the last time, get off that bloody computer" Or worse, do you go head to head with your child and in a blinding moment of rage grab the computer's cord and yank it from the power socket just like Aimee in our scenario did? Do you find yourself going on and on, and lecturing them about their supposed screen mania? Do you think your neurotic attitude towards this also shows some manic traits?

We suggest that you take stock and start to think rather than endlessly react. Do whatever it takes to lose your preoccupation over stomping out the kids' screen-time and stripping them of their dignity. Why? As we've mentioned previously all kids and teens stick close to forbidden fruit. As soon as they fear they're not getting enough, they'll push to get what they can. When it is obvious that we distrust and dislike what they love, we actually drive them to it. As well, when kids sense that you're at war with them, their natural instinct is to battle you and gain ground at all cost. You know this anyway, don't you? We've got one last question that might help you gauge whether you're a 'screen Nazi'. When something goes wrong is your first instinct to withdraw screen privileges from your child?

Highlight alternate activities

Getting off the computer when time is up is hard for kids. We know that it's doubly hard for some because they haven't got anything worth moving to that might match the level of engagement they feel while playing on a screen. To help ease them away from the game create a list of attractive things they could do instead of playing on the computer. Take a look at the chapter, 'Mum, I'm bored!' Here, you'll find 57 fabulous boredom antidotes, and some of these may just do the trick! Another option, providing they have a little screen-time left, may be to move from the computer to the television to watch a favourite program recorded earlier.

Establish expectations early

Those who know tell us that it's best to keep kids virtually screen free during the first three years of their lives. Then gradually introduce screens, and extend time based on the kids' capacity to handle it and respect family rules. Be very clear about how much screen-time is available to each child each day.

If your child pushes for more, don't give in. Instead, be practical and explain to them the behaviours they need to be showing in order to have more screen-time. As with all things at home, rules work best when the kids have been involved making them and when the result is a reasonable representation of their opinions. Make compromises and make it win/win for everyone.

Shared screens in shared spaces

Right from the start, locate the computer(s) in a shared area of the family home. By doing so, you'll have the best chance to monitor their use. Sharing a computer is super social training because as we share we learn to become mindful of the needs of others. The flip side to sharing screens in a shared space is to supply each of the kids a bunch of screens with internet access and set them up to use them in their bedrooms behind closed doors. For some parents, this is the most reliable babysitter money can buy, and yet, these very same parents have the audacity to complain that their children are addicted to screens.

If your child already has a pack of screens freely available to them in their bedroom, we've got to ask, "What were you thinking?" You know it's never too late to make adjustments and introduce the idea that screens are expected to be used in shared spaces. Sometimes, just by relocating the computer from a child's bedroom is enough to reduce their screen usage.

Sharing a computer is super social training because as we share we learn to become mindful of the needs of others.

Timetables and schedules

To simplify the sharing of screens, create a timetable with the kids so they know how much time they can spend on various screens each day, and when. Be sure that the time they are given for video games is reasonable because it is frustrating to just get started and then have to turn the game off. We suggest about thirty minutes. Also consider how you might break their screen-time up into several parcels of twenty to thirty minutes, rather than being with the screen for an hour and a half nonstop.

Having a permanent visual reminder to glance at is a wonderful little life saver. Not only does it help to regulate the amount of screen time, but most kids take comfort in having a computer timetable because it provides a sense of security. So, once you've built a timetable stick with it! The other bonus is that it becomes so much easier to keep track of the number of hours the kids are on screens each week.

The rule of thumb for most of the families we work with is not to schedule screens during mornings before school. Screens stay off as there's always a lot to do. In a few cases, parents will introduce a short screen-time before school as an incentive for kids to stick with the before school routine. Try it by all means, but be prepared to drop it if it doesn't pay results. Most families build screen-time into weekday afternoons, mixed in with a range of other activities. Our cleverest families create a 'golden rule' and stick to it. That is, for a child to receive their allotted screen-time they must have cooperated in the morning as they prepared for school and have had a fair go at any homework.

There can be social costs for kids when screen-time is cut

The fact is that most kids have friends and acquaintances at school and online, so if you're considering winding back online time you'll need to consider the impact this may have on their relationships. Ask them how shorter bursts of time will impact on games, especially if they are part of a team. Accept the very real possibility that your child may be criticized when those from their online community notice that they aren't online as much. There aren't easy answers. One thing we do know is that your child will appreciate you understanding that screens can be an important part of their social world.

My child's online life gives them all the social connections they need

A deluded few argue that some kids blossom socially in the freedom and anonymity of online lives in games and in chat rooms. Our response is that kids need to have real lives independent of their cyber ones in order to develop socially, emotionally, and physically. They need a complete set of interpersonal skills that an exclusive online life cannot provide.

Time limits

Even with a perfectly colour coded timetable setting out various screen-options for each of the kids at precise times each day of the week - you'll still run into problems. The problems usually relate to time limits. That's right, even though the start and finish time can be seen on the timetable, finishing up gracefully and on time, can be a problem for lots of kids. So, let's think ahead and plan for this highly likely contingency. Here are a few ideas to help kids stay within time limits;

Set a stopwatch or the kitchen timer as they begin

Be sure that you and your child can hear it when it finally sounds! For younger kids, find a timer that helps them see how much time is left. Sand or goo-timers are perfect. Otherwise google 'audible timers' and be amazed! These are electronic and they display the passing of time and can tell you how much is left in five minute increments. They're inexpensive too.

"But I'm in the middle of the game!"

When the timer goes off you're likely to hear, "But I'm in the middle of the game!" Prepare for this. Almost every game has a save game function, so your child can pause or save in the middle of a game without losing any points, clues, weapons, resources and so on. You may have to help them work out how this function works. It's a good investment to sit with the kids sometimes as they play their game. By doing this you'll understand what the game is about, why they like it, why they get so involved and how it works. We suggest that games without save points (or games designed to get to specific places before you can save) are only played on the weekend.

Chat room sites

Likewise, your kids will enter a phase where they like chat room sites or enjoy chatting with others as they play a game. In most cases, these will not cause worry. Our advice is to sit with them in the beginning, and coach them how to handle this new experience. Teach them how to be safe and sensible and work within time limits.

Use music as a reminder

Cue your kids into the time they have by using music. Select a mix of their favourite songs so that the length of the music matches the amount of computer time they have.

Be playful

When it's time for them to get off the screen, say it in a funny way rather than using your usual voice that may be interpreted by them as nagging. Walk past and give them a cuddle as you say, "Time's up in 5 minutes". Or be silent and pop a note in front of them that says, "Five minutes to go". Just for fun, send older kids an affectionate text message to remind them their time's up - "Time's up. Meet me in the kitchen for a smoothie!"

Banking time

Always permit kids to bank or save up extra chunks of screen-time when they've left the screen early, especially when you've had to ask them to leave early and they've acquiesced.

Bedtime

It's wise to give young teens more time and let them use the computer later in the evening. However, keep in mind that researchers consistently say screens should be switched of at least forty-five minutes before bed time.

Chapter 8:

"Get off that computer, now!"

What should I do when they won't get off the computer?

Our challenge throughout this book is to have you shower your attention on the behaviours you want to see more of, because attention always strengthens behaviour. That's right - give little attention and emotion to what you don't want more of and, as you do this, the behaviour that you don't like will diminish over time. So, how might this look when your child won't get off the computer? It is deceptively simple.

Case study...

You might say, "Bond, it's time to finish up on the computer in ten minutes." Next comes the five minute warning, "Bond, you've got five minutes left and then come for dinner!" When time is up so you say, "Come on kiddo, dinner's on the table. You've got two minutes to be here or you lose your screen-time tomorrow."

That's it! That's all you need to say.

Be sure to follow this consequence through matter-of-factly without scowling, gloating, going on and on or showing annoyance when Bond arrives late to the table. When Bond does arrive you might say, "Mate, you know the deal. When it's time to get off the computer you need to listen and do it. You didn't do that today, so tomorrow there's no screen-time."

If you need to, quietly move away from Bond. If you're confronted with a temper tantrum stay calm and do not buy into it. What you want to reinforce in an emotionally steady manner is that Bond made a poor choice, and because of this, he will be miss out on screen-time tomorrow. Keep it this simple, and persist.

What about when stronger parental control is necessary?

Let's state the obvious - 'no tool will ever replace the skillful supervision of parents.' The best security you can have is your child's trust about what's wise and unwise to do online, on screens, and why. Keeping open communication about how the kids use screens and the internet is a much better option than blocking their access.

If you must use a stronger level of control, then go into the control panel on the computer. Click on 'user accounts and family safety', and then click on user accounts. Once you're here, it should bring up the account that you're currently on. You can add a password that that will be required to access the computer. By doing so you have control over when the kids can play. From now on your children will have to ask in order to use the computer. Also, there's a host of inexpensive parental control software that can restrict, filter and monitor the use of the computer. Programs such as

TimesUpKidz , WebWatcher, Ez Internet Timer and SpyAgent are popular to mention just a few. Once they're set, they'll limit the time your kids can spend on the computer by defining the time of day available to each of them.

How important are video game classifications?

We're staggered by the number of parents who ignore classification ratings on video games and allow their kids to play violent, first person shooter games for hours on end. Such games plunge young brains into role-play situations where the darkest aspects of humanity are played out

with graphics so life-like that it pales the hard hitting six o'clock news into insignificance. We have known for years that violent video games increase aggression related thoughts and decreases helping behaviour in some children and young adults (Anderson, 2001). We've also learnt that those who are overexposed to video game violence are more likely to be involved in physical fights, to get into arguments with teachers more often, and perform poorly in school (Gentile, 2004).

So, armed with this easily available knowledge why is it that there remain a hard core group of parents who ignore video game classifications? In our work, we're seeing too many children, as young as seven and eight years of age, regularly playing M and MA15+ rated games. In a few instances where parents refuse to entertain the connection between their child obsessing over the video game and acting out the violent video action at school and home, a mandatory report to a child protection agency is the only course of action to help them to take stock.

Should daily access to screens be a child's right?

Absolutely not!

Whether they appreciate it or not, our kids rely on our wisdom to guide them in safe and balanced directions. Our surveying of parents reveal that just over a third with children aged ten years allow them up to two hours of screen-time each day on weekends, but offer no screen-time for games on school days. Correspondingly, just under a third of parents with children aged ten give their kids a free run on screens every day of the week. They tell us that their children spend much more than two hours on screens most days.

Here's our take on it. We think it's unwise to cultivate a custom where kids plug into a screen at will. We advocate three provisos for kids and teens;

Provision one

Screen-time needs to be earned by way of being thoughtful, cooperative and helpful. Homework tasks, the before school routine and daily chores have to be done before screens are switched on. To illustrate this, one of our clever families offers each of their boys three tokens throughout the day. Each token is worth fifteen minutes on a screen later in the day. The first token is achieved when the boys follow the morning routine and are ready for school on time. The second is earned when the boys unpack their schoolbags, place notices and lunchboxes on the kitchen bench, change out of their school uniform and start their homework. The final token is handed over when each of the boys has completed their homework. This works so much better than constantly nagging and correcting behaviour. The idea has great potential to be adapted and used in all kinds of other ways.

Provision two

The kids must ask before they turn a screen on. While you will usually say, "yes" if it's in the agreed time, and they've earned it, asking is a simple courtesy to keep you informed about what they're doing. By developing the expectation that they need to check in with you before a screen is flicked on, you circumvent them believing screen-time is their undeniable right?

Provision three

If your child is not able to finish up their screen-time, on time and with grace, they would always lose their screen-time the following day.

Teach teens how to multitask

Like it or not, most teens chat online, play a game, check out 'facebook' and listen to music while they do homework. That's the reality! It's not really understood what affect this style of multitasking has on how people learn, but we do know that it will take them longer to do their homework. Accept that they will multitask in this way - just as you do! Teach them how to do it and how they might monitor their progress, rather than taking a hard line demanding they cannot multitask in this way. Most teens get their heads around this with astute support from parents. For a few, especially the immature and those with obsessional patterns of thinking, this is a much harder road for parents to tread. These teens rely on parents to help them self-regulate because they're not able to do this themselves.

Chapter 8:

"Get off that computer, now!"

The 'facebook' screen

We couldn't write this chapter without mentioning 'facebook', as currently it's such a popular screen for so many of our young clients. 'facebook' says users must be at least thirteen years old, but that doesn't stop younger kids from joining because all they have to do is lie about their age. Many kids use it, and use a number of other social networking sites, without the knowledge or care of their parents. 'facebook' claims to have controls that monitor the so-called friends on children's accounts, manage the privacy controls and limit the applications kids use, but these are inadequate and provide nowhere near the safety a helpful parent can. As long as there are mechanisms in place by parents to protect kids, we see it as a reasonable platform for young teens to keep in touch with friends and extended family. However to keep your kids safe here's what we suggest;

The password

The password gives full access to your child's profile. It must be shared with a parent and no one else. This permits parents to check the news feed and inbox every so often. To us, this has to be a permanent rule.

You must be your child's friend

Parents and kids must be 'facebook friends'. Parents must be able to view all pictures, videos, posts, updates, tags… everything! This helps to keep kids safe, their reputations intact and minimises unwanted surprises.

Responsibility

While kids can't be completely responsible for silly or offensive things their friends post on their wall, they are responsible for anything posted from their own profile. If they allow a friend to use their profile to send messages out to people, your child is responsible for it. Once something is posted, it can never be permanently erased from the system and can be used as evidence in disputes.

Others watch

What your child posts may eventually be seen by everyone - brothers, sisters, friends, fathers, principals, youth leaders, teachers, family friends, neighbours and the police. Whenever your kids post something, teach them to ask themselves, "Would I be happy if my principal, teacher or grandmother saw this?"

Friends

'facebook' is all about connecting people. Work with your kids to avoid 'friending' people just because they want more friends, and never 'friend' a stranger. The key questions when considering friend requests are, "do I really trust this person to see my updates, my pictures and the information I post? Am I sure this person will not do something stupid or mean with them?"

Conflicts

Encourage kids to take online conflicts into the real world. If you witness the breakdown of a relationship because of angry or thoughtless words posted online, encourage your teen to sort it out, preferably face to face. If things are really out of hand, be proactive and call your child's school or the other parents to give them the best chance to sort it through. Our brains are still wired for face to face social exchange and things can go seriously wrong when we have to make guesses about other's emotional states.

Personal information can become public

Sadly, there are bad people in the world who want to do harm to others. They hack 'facebook' accounts to gain access to people's private information. To remain safe, never post personal information - physical address, full birth date, school and so on. Never write updates such as, "Parents are gone" or "I'm home alone and bored," Such statements invite devious people to do malicious things.

When worried, ask for help

Participating in an online social network opens up all kinds of new situations for people to deal with. Even experienced adults run into trouble from time to time. So expect your kids to run into tricky scenarios every so often. Every child on 'facebook' needs a safe place to turn when a rough time emerges. That safe place should be their mother or father.

My Notes:

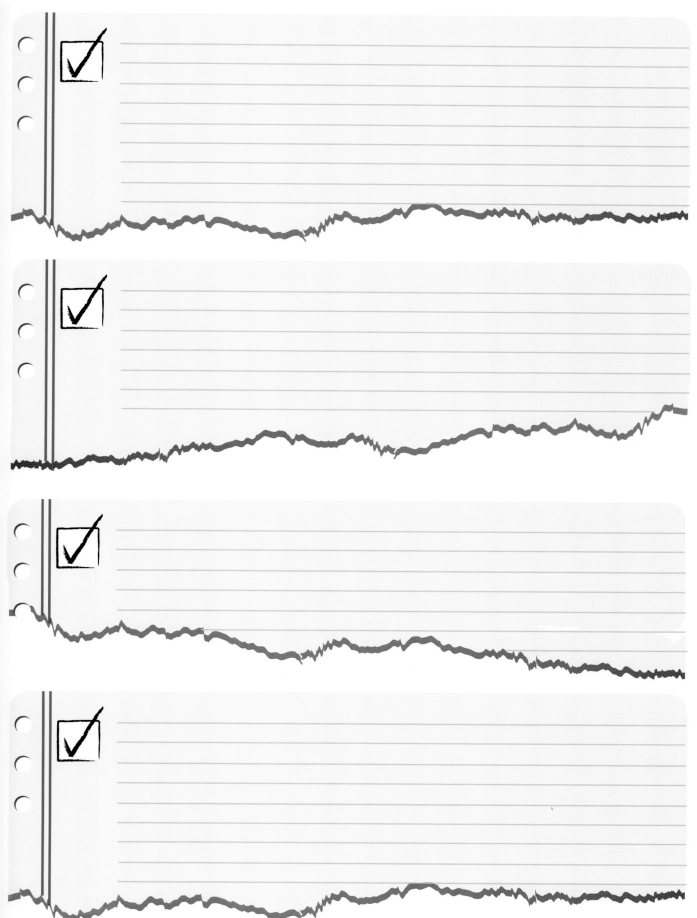

Ingredients:

- A child calling, "Mum, I'm bored"
- A child who expects mum or dad to fix their boredom
- A parent who jumps into action because they think their job is to be their children's entertainment director
- A spoilt child who gets whatever they want
- A child with poor independent skills, a short concentration span and pushes to be on the go
- A parent tired of finding things to keep the kids busy
- A parent who complains, but secretly feels fulfilled by the act of amusing their children

Recipe rescue:

clever ideas to deal with kid's boredom

The scenario...

"Mum, I'm bored"

It's Saturday morning. The kids woke early so we stuck them in front of the television. Our hope was to grab a few moments back in bed and read the paper with a coffee. Two minutes after jumping back into bed, our ten year old son yells, "This is boring. I'm going on the XBox to play my new game." He knows XBox times are restricted and that I regret buying him this latest game - it's too violent and he's already addicted! I call out, "No, leave the XBox alone. Go and do something else."

"There isn't anything else to do....
"Mum, I'm bored."

My heart sinks. Boredom would be a luxury for me! In the few remaining moments I have left in bed,

I contemplate what, "Mum, I'm bored" really means. Does it mean, "I'm too lazy to do anything except complain", "Give me your undivided attention", "You do the thinking for me" or, "Come on, keep me entertained."

Would I be better off ignoring him or responding with something like;

"You're bored because you're boring."
"That's because you're tired. Go back to sleep."
"Well, now's the time to catch up on that homework"
"Hey, here's a damp cloth, go to the lounge and dust the skirting boards"

Is it wrong for kids to feel bored?

How can kids today possibly be bored? They've got everything imaginable to amuse them. They have unlimited entertainment available - free to air TV, pay TV, smartphones, wii, Xbox, Nintendo 3DS, iPads, iPods, Surface and thousands of inexpensive games from the internet ready for immediate download! What's more, they have toys we could have only imagined as kids - Lego, Lego robotics, motorised scooters, kick scooters, skateboards, bikes, remote controlled cars, trucks, helicopters and planes and so on and so on and so on. Yet our kids still come to us and say they're bored. What if we were to raise a few thoughts at this point?

A few points worth considering about boredom from Bill and Mark

☑ There's nothing wrong with being bored sometimes.

☑ Boredom is a very normal human emotion as genuine as happiness or sadness – it has its place.

☑ We have to learn to deal with boredom, just as we learn to deal with other emotions.

☑ Boredom is a valuable teacher - it helps us to learn to be by ourselves, to ponder, imagine and even reconstruct past experiences in order to build better futures.

☑ "Mum, I'm bored" means many things, such as - "I feel tired", "Let me play on the computer", "Can I go to the movies" or "I don't feel like doing much at the moment."

☑ Your child's boredom can sometimes be an invitation for you to connect with them.

Funnily enough there's also a line of thought where some parents see kids' boredom as a 'crime'. Consequently, "Mum, I'm bored" is sarcastically countered with, "Then go sweep the kitchen," or "I wish I was lucky enough to feel bored" or "You can't be bored. You have hundreds of toys" or "Suck it up, princess!" We propose that the tradition of dismissing kids or belittling kids when they say they're bored deserves a second thought. We believe children and young teens deserve a thoughtful and respectful response. If you're ready for this, then you'll enjoy our Recipe rescue. It encourages healthier ways to think about your children's boredom, and what to do with it.

Recipe rescue:

clever ideas to deal with kid's boredom

If *"Mum, I'm bored"* drives you mad then it's time to review the role you play in this.

All those extracurricular activities may be lowering your child's boredom tolerance

Most of us try hard to keep our kids busily engaged in extra activities outside of school to meet their aspirations, interests and talents. It's what we do as parents. We're driven to give them the best opportunities we can, and there's nothing wrong with wanting to give them the best.

But, what is best? Does the fact that many of us deliver a smorgasbord of entertainment impact on how our kids respond to the quieter times in their lives? None of us want to be accused of hothouse-styled parenting, but one can't help wonder whether the intensity we apply to our kid's extracurricular activities is stealing some of the joys of childhood - downtime, day-dream time, alone time and having time to mooch, muse and create. The truth is that our kid's lives don't always have to be full, busy and striving. Running our kids ragged with full-time extracurricular activities won't make their childhoods better. If anything, it may very well work to lower their boredom tolerance.

Screen 'addiction' and boredom

If you think your child has too much 'screen time' and seems to be pushing for more, then think about the role you're playing in this. Things tend not to happen in isolation - are you a gamer, an avid facebooker, a compulsive tweeter, a phone addict, or worse still, behave like a 'screen time' Nazi? Yes, a child's push for more and more screen time is directly related to our own habits and attitudes, and how we use and feel about them. Most of us would admit in the privacy of this moment that we're guilty of using screens as babysitters way too often. After all, screens are a handy way to keep squabbling kids separate, to keep them amused, or to give the family respite from a difficult kid. If you think your kids have too much 'screen time' begin the winds of change by modelling healthy behaviour yourself. As of today, invent a new term called, "screen rubbish". This term describes the difference between screens that have some kind of an intellectual or educational bias, compared to fast trigger entertainment! Secondly, develop some sensible family 'screen time' rules. Health experts warn us it's best not to expose children under the age of 3 years to screens at all! The sensible thinking is to increase 'screen time' very, very gradually to a maximum of 2 hours per day for 12 year olds.

'Screen time' always needs to be earned, always broken up into thirty minute portions, always located in a shared space and always switched off an hour before going to sleep. We're not saying it's easy. And, we beg you not to become a blatant 'Screen Nazi'.

Kids stick close to forbidden fruit. When they know we distrust and dislike what they love, we actually drive them to it. The impact of technology on us is truly brave new world stuff! Our brains have never been subjected to the amount of cognitive input that's coming at us, and you can't switch off the world. All you can do is educate yourself, along with your children, to manage this better.

We see too many children with unlimited access to all kinds of 'screens'. The result is nothing short of screen addiction. But, why would anyone be surprised? Online and screen mediums bombard the brain with super visual and auditory stimuli. It is so powerful that while engaged, our brains set up a tantalizing positive feedback loop. Even supposedly simple acts as receiving a text message are considered rewards by the brain - yes, like a hit from a drug - and of course, more is better! Kids who are constantly plugged in become used to a 'screen time' reward pattern that's more enticing than what they experience in the real world.

The consequence of screen addiction sees people of all ages finding it difficult to tolerate any 'down time'. Real life gradually takes on an under-stimulating and under-whelming feel when compared to virtual world. So, what do they do? You've seen them. You may even do it yourself. They reach for their smartphones or gadgets the moment they are not directly engaged in a conversation, while they're walking, shopping, at the checkout, as soon as they're waiting at the bus stop, when driving or even while sitting on the toilet! There is no room for 'down time' in their lives anymore; they have rewired their brains so the scope for healthy boredom no longer exists.

If you think your kids have too much 'screen time' begin the winds of change by modelling healthy behaviour yourself.... Yes, a child's push for more and more screen time is directly related to our own habits and attitudes, and how we use and feel about them.

Let's rethink, "Mum, I'm bored"

The word **bored** is ambiguous. It can mean different things to different kids at different times - recognise this and tune into it. We need to be clever translators.

So from now on, when you hear "Mum, I'm bored" ask your child;

- **What made you bored?**
- **Being bored is okay. You know that don't you?**
- **It's an odd feeling, isn't it? Got any ideas?**
- **Are you okay to just hang around for a while?**
- **That's just your clever brain sorting out how to do something more quietly. It will come up with something to do. Let me know when it does, okay?**

At home: "Mum, I'm bored" could mean;

- **I want to spend some time with you**
- **I need you to tell me what I should do**
- **I don't like what I'm doing right now**
- **I feel sick**
- **I want to do something that I know you won't really agree to**
- **I want to go on the computer to play my game**
- **I want you to organise something that I'll enjoy**
- **I'm just at a loose end**

About school: "Mum, I'm bored" could mean;

- **I want to spend some time with you**
- **The work is too hard**
- **The work is too easy**
- **I haven't had enough sleep and I'm tired**
- **The day is too long**
- **I can't read or write like the others**
- **I haven't got friends**
- **Kids are being mean to me**
- **I'm not getting my way**
- **My teacher screams or is bossy**

What to do when your child says, "Mum, I'm bored"

Is it our job to always relieve our kid's boredom? Of course not! Our call to duty is to be shrewd and invent systems with our kids so that when boredom crops up, there are appetizing options they're attracted to. One idea is to get busy and generate a short list of 'Things to do when I feel bored'. Develop a wall chart and display it in a conspicuous position. Divide the chart into two columns. One column for the things kids can 'do alone' and the other for things the kids can 'do with each other'. Try not to overwhelm kids with too many choices. Instead, have just 5 delicious choices in each column and be prepared to update the list every three months or so.

Alternatively, make a 'Boredom-dare jar'.

To do this get a large plastic jar or cheap goldfish bowl. Then fill it with a host of activities, challenges and dares - each one written on a folded sheet of paper. You've got the idea, this is lucky dip style for the kids - some of the activities are fun, some will demand the kids entertain you, some will have you entertaining them, some will deliver an unexpected delight, others will ask them to do a chore, something challenging or something bizarre.

Chapter 9:

"Mum, I'm bored!"

To get you off to a great start here's some fabulous boredom antidotes. These ideas are not meant to be an overwhelming dump of ideas. See them as delightful choices and only choose a few at a time that you know will appeal. These choices then become the focus when the kids are feeling bored. Oh, you'll notice that we haven't included anything to do with 'screens'. That's deliberate because 'screens' tend to happen anyway! Enjoy;

"Mum, I'm bored!" IDEAS:

1. Go and play netball, basketball, soccer, football, cricket, tennis or practice any sporting skill
2. Set up a beep test, pull out your score card and try to improve on previous times
3. Go practice your instrument - piano, drums, guitar, etc.
4. Listen to music, write a playlist for bored moments
5. Build a tent in the backyard ready to camp out later on
6. Go jump on the trampoline - it's a great way to positively change mood states!
7. Read a book, a comic or a magazine
8. Write a story and make a book or a comic from it
9. Build a marble run or a fabulous domino run - then let them fall
10. Do a colouring-in or paint by number activity
11. Do some mazes from a giant maze book or make your own mazes for others to solve later on
12. Get the bowling pins out and start a bowling competition with yourself or with others
13. Take a long, long bubble bath and cut your toenails and fingernails
14. Create and practice a puppet show to show to the family later on
15. Film yourself acting something from a book, talking with your pets, singing a song or making a documentary. Show it to everyone later. Keep a file of these as part of family records
16. Make a card or write a letter to a friend or family member
17. Go take some great photos
18. Use duct tape and cardboard boxes to build something
19. Have fun blowing bubbles
20. Make something with clay, plasticine or play-doh
21. Play cards - Go Fish, Solitaire, Old Maid, Snap, Concentration or War
22. Build a house of cards and set a record for height or cards used for next time
23. Phone a friend or a relative and talk
24. Count the money in your moneybox or Moonjar
25. Go and look under the seats in the house and in the car for coins - make sure you plant a few!
26. Get outside and catch a little critter. Research it and build it a habitat for it
27. Go and get the skipping rope and skip and skip and skip
28. Paint or finger-paint. Never forget shaving cream on coloured paper!
29. Design place mats for each person for the dinner table
30. Design a treasure hunt for the family for later
31. Play hide and seek
32. Build a commando course and set it up for everyone to use later
33. Have fun playing in the sprinkler
34. Target practice using 'nerf guns' or similar
35. Draw on the path with chalk
36. Organise and have a picnic in the backyard
37. Take the dog for a walk
38. Do a puzzle or board game - Carcassonne for Kids, Go Nuts! Scrabble, Magic Labyrinth, Minotaurus Ring-O Flamingo, Chutes and Ladders, Candyland, Pay Day, Trouble, Sorry, Monopoly, etc.
39. Throw a Frisbee
40. Cut out paper snowflakes, paper designs or paper dolls
41. Face paint each other or do it to yourself in the mirror
42. Play hangman
43. Check out insects with a magnifying glass
44. Ask mum or dad if you can do a job around the house for money or to surprise them
45. Go ride your rollerblades, skates, skateboard or your bike
46. Get the Lego out and start building!

"Mum, I'm bored!" IDEAS:

47. Re-organise a bit of your bedroom
48. Give the dog a bath
49. Water the vegetable garden or plant some new ones
50. Open up a packet of balloons; play air soccer or fill them up with water ready for a balloon fight
51. Get building with bits of wood, a hammer and nails

52. Squeeze some oranges or lemons and set up a shop at the front of your house with advertising
53. Have a funny face competition. Make funny faces and photograph the best faces!
54. Get out the dress ups, dress up and photograph the best ready to show everyone later
55. Carve a small boat from balsa wood and see if it floats. How much can it carry?

Next time you hear your child shriek, "Mum, I'm bored" try to remember when you were their age. Can you recall thinking, "I don't know what to" or "I haven't got anyone to play with" or "What could I do in this house, on a day like this?" but the words that flew out of your mouth were, "Mum, I'm bored". In reality you were at a loose end. There were probably a lot of things you could have done, but needed a kick start to engage in something.

We think it's best to develop a simple, but ever evolving 'anti-boredom plan' together. In this way, the kids can use their bored feeling as a motivation to attach to another activity. It is a matter of helping them take the first step away from boredom - into engagement while everyone keeps their dignity. It's also a way to set up new habits.

As well, there are a few basic guidelines to keep in mind. First, it is natural for younger children to have shorter concentration spans, be more impulsive and rely on others for their stimulation.

Secondly, some children need to be taught 'how-to engage in tasks'. This begins with us modelling how we engage, stick with enjoy, and finish tasks. Yes, our kids watch our every move so never discount the power of role-modelling how you engage and get pleasure from simple activities. Finally, when you have the time, start your kids off on an activity with you playing as well. Gently guide and coach them how to play, how to enjoy and how to be absorbed in something.

Ingredients:

- A typical challenging life situation at hand
- An emotionally overwhelmed child
- A parent who wants to help
- A parent anxious to shield their child from life's bumps
- A parent who striving to make their child's life problem free
- A parent without a realistic long term plan

Recipe rescue:

being the best resilience coach for your kids

The scenarios:

Good advice, or is it?

I try and try to help my eight year old son not to be so sad or reactive when things go wrong, but my advice falls on deaf ears. He says, "I've tried that", "I'm not doing that", "that's stupid", and "that won't work". All I want is for him to be happy, but I'm not making any headway. Sometimes, I think he wears his attitude as a badge of honour.

"What happened at school today? Were you okay?"

I've talked to the teacher countless times about the friendship problems my twelve year old daughter has. She and the school counsellor don't get to see what I sense. They think Amie is happy with friends at school and that I'm a serial worrier. All I want to do is protect her! Every afternoon when I ask, "what happened today?" there's another upsetting story. Lately, we both end up in tears!

Her moods control the weather

When something doesn't work out at school our thirteen year old arrives home with dark storm clouds around her. She's quick to play the victim. She blames everyone else. Her moods control the weather in our house, making our world a much darker place. The more I tell her to see the optimistic side, the worse she gets. I worry about her inability to bounce back. I also worry that her constant pessimism may lead to depression.

Hours of talking may not be an answer

Most nights, as my ten year old daughter settles into bed, she wants to discuss what's happened during the day. The recurrent theme is about unfair encounters with teachers and the ups and downs that go with friendship. We talk for hours! Lately, I've been bringing out the oil and massaging her back while we dissect issue by issue. She loves this. Trouble is that these encounters are becoming more regular and her problems are increasing despite hours of talking.

What is resilience?

It's got to be important. After all, thousands of presenters and franchisees woo us with programs purported to build the resilience of young people. Resilience building programs have become a billion dollar industry and they abound with variable degrees of credibility and effectiveness.

Why is resilience such a prized quality?

Resiliency is a measure of a person's capacity to bounce-back, optimistically and constructively, from the inevitable challenges life consistently throws at each of us for as long as we live.

Resilient qualities

Someone who...

- sees life's disappointments as challenges rather than awful stressors
- can 'switch on' confidence, kindness and determination when needed
- can set goals and follow them through

- has a realistic sense of balance between their strengths and challenges
- can have a good laugh at themselves at times
- shares, listens and is able to place practical advice into constructive action
- enjoys connecting with others
- likes to help and be reassuring to others

So, there you have it - a point of reference for what resilient qualities are.

How resilient are you?

- ☑ Are you an optimist?
- ☑ How resilient were your parents?
- ☑ Did you inherit their bounce-back?
- ☑ How resilient are you compared to your brothers and sisters?
- ☑ Are you more resilient now than you were as a child?
- ☑ Have you experienced events that have strengthened your resiliency?
- ☑ Can you identify these events?
- ☑ Why is it that you're able to bounce back from some situations, but not so well from others?
- ☑ Do your friendships encourage or reduce your resilience?

As you ponder these questions, you'll appreciate that resilience is a complex and elusive quality. Resilience building involves a life time worth of experiences, maturation and reflection. Yet, we remain astonished by a steady stream of parents who believe it must be possible for someone else - a program or a therapist - to magically 'top up' their child's resilience.

Resilience – a context

'L-plates'

By virtue of their age kids are inexperienced. They haven't yet learnt to smoothly process everything that comes their way and express feelings predictably and appropriately. Yet at the same time, they participate in rich and lively emotional lives. Consequently, emotional upsets and wobbly times are bound to occur - that's just a fact of life!

Reflect - it's never too late to change

Some of us know that we're not as resilient as we'd like to be and remain upset by memories of an emotionally vulnerable childhood. That's why it's frightening to see the same susceptible traits in our precious kids! These traits fill us with fear, and before we know it, our love has us over-helping and fixing things up for them. Little by little, our overprotectiveness creates a helpless child - the very thing we wanted to avoid. Without reflection we can become one of the greatest barriers to our children's healthy emotional development.

The good news is that it's never too late to change our habits. You know where a large part of your resilience has come from, don't you? It's the memory that you faced a problem or setback like this before, did it tough, hurt for a bit, recaptured your composure, conquered the problem and gained confidence. The same applies for kids. It's a tough gig, but our kids need us to step up by sometimes stepping back.

A complicated recipe

Assisting children to build resilience is complicated, and demands a plan. Resilience slowly builds in the same way we'd carefully build a thirty five layered napoleon cake. Resilience is the icing on the top of the cake and it's the result of all the hard underpinning work put into the build. It takes thought, time and care.

We're their best models!

If we expect kids to think and perform resiliently, then we've got to model it ourselves - there's no other way. Parents who are able show constructive responses to life's problems, especially when under pressure, drip-feed a powerful behavioural message about resilience to their children. The best thing we can do is to show our kids how-to handle their feelings by handling our own really well.

Recipe rescue:

being the best resilience coach for your kids

The 10 C's at a Glance:

C1: **Competence**

C2: **Confidence**

C3: **Connection**

C4: **Conversion**

C5: **Contribution**

C6: **Coping**

C7: **Control**

C8: **Communication**

C9: **Competition**

C10: **Common sense**

This Recipe rescue examines the ordinary, everyday things we can do to promote resilient attitudes in our children. While there's not an elixir to guarantee the healthiest of emotional futures, there are some common sense principles to maximise emerging resilient qualities in young people. We call them 'the 10C's' - 10 resilient competencies worth knowing and drawing from to coach kids.

C1: Competence

Coach kids to build 'can do' attitudes when faced with tricky situations. Encourage a positive problem-solving attitude and inspire them to make a choice even if it involves taking a sensible risk. Engage them to think about different solutions and possible courses of action. When errors of judgement happen, and they will, use the mistake as an opportunity to for them to learn and grow. Mistakes are okay - having a red hot go matters most! When children develop plans of action through the guidance of parents, their sense of competence grows.

C2: Confidence

When parents radiate accepting signals about their children, they place them in the best position to feel secure and display buoyant thinking. Each of your children has a set of unique personal qualities - fairness, gentleness, reliability, persistence, determination, lovingness, loyalty, honesty or kindness. When they handle a tricky situation well, tell them the resilient quality you saw shine through. They need to know that they have it so they are more likely to use it in the future. Try planting a 'seed of confidence' next time your child discusses a challenging situation with you. It might go something like this, "That sounds tough, but you always persist and I know you'll stick with this till the end". Plant that vital seed into your child's psyche!

The tougher part of this confidence building equation is accepting your child when they show idiosyncrasies, anxieties and behaviours that are tough to live with. This is our call to step up, and acknowledge that the basic personality of our kids can be shaped - well, a little - but, not a lot. Of far greater value is to help them identify what Loretta Giorcelli named, 'Islands of competence' (http://www.doctorg.org/). A strong marker of resilience is when an individual can identify areas of their lives they feel skilled or positive about. Work with your kids to develop an 'Island of competence' inventory. It's as simple as asking them to draw their fantasy island, write their name on to it, add some colour, attach a photo of themselves and help them create a list of their unique personal qualities, skills and interests. Display each of their 'Islands' in a prominent place and arrange that you will sign off and write spectacular comments next to the quality when you see them use it. Without maintaining an 'Island of competence' approach is too easy to let the usual tricky things be swallowed up by continents of incompetence!

C3: Connection

We know, unquestionably, that the quality of a mother's and father's connection with each of their children is crucial to their intellectual, social and emotional development. This of course is the tenant of this book. The reoccurring theme is to do all you can to develop connectedness and build a solid sense of family, attachment and security. Just as vital, is your child's connection to other children. Read the literature - it's conclusive. The higher the quality of relationship our kids experience with other kids, the greater the chances of solid emotional health. And, sound emotional health is a prerequisite for resilient thinking. This doesn't mean you must become obsessed by arranging endless 'play-dates' for your child. It all about quality, not quantity!

Despite the finest of intentions by parents and teachers, school isn't always a good place for all kids to find and feel friendship. Some kids just take longer to build their social muscle and rely on us to think outside of the square to engineer friendly connections.

Formal social skills programs

A formal social skills training program (www.*whatsthebuzz*.net.au) teaches children, as part of a group, how-to become a positive problem solver, how-to be a friend, what it feels like to laugh with and feel friendship, to understand more about themselves and how-to think resiliently. The best gains are made with continuing input from home and school - the right prompts, the right language and cueing.

Informal social connections

Having a friend over to play with your child is a sensible option to gently explore. Initially, keep visits short, structured and one on one. If you must, get rid of the pesky little brother or sister! Remember, younger children require a lot more adult direction.

Community connections

For some, the best chance to develop social connections takes place where they are able to be with others over a common interest. So, gather up the contacts of clubs, associations, groups and organisations. They can play a wonderful role to improve your child's confidence, esteem and relationship. There are a myriad of groups within the community worth exploring - Joeys, Cubs, Scouts, dance, drama, guinea pig clubs, cat clubs, dog clubs, and so on.

The reoccurring theme is to do all you can to develop connectedness and build a solid sense of family, attachment and security. Just as vital, is your child's connection to other children.

C4: Conversion

Every one of us draws on a 'negative script' with our kids every so often. This is when we use language that's harmful. While our 'negative script' is may be triggered by our anxieties, fears and care, it actively limits our kids' resilience! A perfect example is when we ask, "Oh? How was school today?" and it has that underlying investigative tone ready to sniff out any possible misfortunes our little victim may have suffered.

"Did anyone upset you?"
"Were you happy today?"
"Did you have anyone to play with?"
"Were they okay with you?"
"Were you teased?"
"Did anything happen that I should know about?"

"How was school today?" is such a vague question anyway - never ask it. Every day at school is big because so much happens. It's hard for kids to pick out important bits to chat about, and as a result, it's easier for them to dwell on negative aspects or to roll their eyes at you and shut down. It doesn't take long for our kids to learn that these questions are all about our anxiety and low confidence in them. Very quickly they will tell you exactly what you expect to hear. If you feel compelled to ask about their day, try;

"What went well today?"
"How did that math homework we did together go? Did I pass?"
"What were you proudest of today?"
"Got anything funny that happened today"
"Did you surprise yourself today?"

Do whatever it takes to convert to 'positive scripts'.

C5: Contribution

When kids are given chances to contribute they gain a sense they can make a difference, and that the world can be a better place because they are in it. Our challenge as parents is to find ways for them to develop concern, compassion and a social conscience.

At home, one way to raise your children's contribution is to organise for them to prepare a meal for the family each week or fortnight. Sure, it may end up making a little extra work for you, but it's a long term investment in their mental health. With help, most five year olds are capable of arranging a simple meal for the family and serving it to them. As we nudge children to do more for others it immerses them into the world of giving. Without this we risk teaching them to believe that the world owes them something. What a devastating shock when they come face to face with reality!

Outside of home, continue to broaden your child's world by arranging 'acts of kindness' they can bestow on others. One option is to involve the family in different forms of help, community or charity work - walks to raise money for hunger, for children with disability or disease, for animal shelters, for the homeless or helping out at the local aged care home. The notion of giving to others immerses them in an emotionally larger world where they can start to compare their attitudes, their life and their feelings to the lives of others. As they see and participate, a more selfless view of life is naturally promoted - no preaching is required.

Finally, ask yourself how long it's been since your child did something to show care for someone who was helpful to them, or to someone who needs their spirits raised? How long is it since your child; made and sent a 'thank you' card, wrote a long newsy letter, mailed a hand-made gift, bought and presented a gift, took some time to make a visit, sent an email or text, wrote and mailed a note or made a telephone call to someone who deserves it? Start by setting them up to deliver a kindness that they may not normally think of. Teaching care to our kids underpins that they themselves are cared for. It teaches how communities receive and contribute.

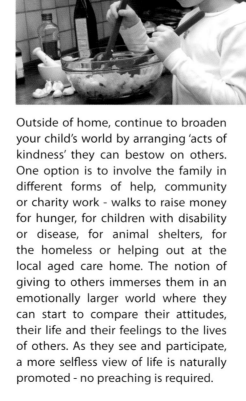

C6: Coping

Tell your kids that although life is wonderful it's not always fair. Tell it right from the start and keep on reminding them in all sorts of ways.

Build positive sayings into everyday life.

Each week offer an optimistic saying to the kids. Leave it on the dining room table and throughout the week ask if anyone was able to do it;

"Wherever you go, no matter what the weather, always bring your own sunshine."
"Every day may not be good, but there's something good in every day."
"Happiness is attitude. We either make ourselves miserable or happy The amount of work is the same."
"Attitude is a little thing that makes a big difference."

Ideal sources for these sayings are inexpensive, inspiring little books often found at local news agencies, or use the internet and Google, 'optimistic sayings'.

Play, 'What if?'

Let's explain - one of your children might mention that their friend, Haydn, got into trouble again at school because …" Here's your chance to play, *'What if?'* You might respond by saying, "Wow, that sounds tricky. Poor Haydn! Hey…

"What if he'd just walked away? What might have happened?"
"What if he had of come and sat with you to talk about it? What might have happened then?"
"What if Haydn had of done something different?"
"What else could have he done?"

These sorts of conversation highlight the fact that choices always exist. They lead children to see how they can think and make good choices.

Rehearse

Discussing how to handle an upcoming event can prevent your child from falling victim to anxious or reactive feelings. So, before heading off to that family gathering, create a plan together. If, for example, a little respite from the action may be helpful arrange for them to withdraw into a quiet room with their DS, iPod touch or to read by themselves or with a friend, for a while. Rehearsing helps all of us to intellectualise what is likely to happen and how we can keep it together.

Teach how-to say sorry

Used well, "sorry" can rescue so many situations! Yet, it's a word that's hard for many to say. Have fun role playing situations where "sorry" would be helpful. Teach them how to show "sorry" in different ways. Help them understand that saying "sorry" isn't admitting that what happened was their fault. It is a signal to heal a problem and restore the relationship.

The 'delete key'

Teach your kids this wonderful visualisation strategy - most love it and will use it! Say to them that sometimes when they feel upset or annoyed by someone they don't need to react. Instead, teach them to press an imaginary 'delete key' or 'shrink key' in their minds. As they do this, those they are having trouble with either disappear or shrink into little babies with smelly nappies. Then, it's so much easier to think, "Hey, it doesn't matter", and walk away."

Think one thing, but say another

Here's a powerful strategy gobbled up by middle primary aged children! Around this age, their new brain connections allow them to think one thing about a difficult person or a troublesome situation, but respond with an entirely different reaction. Suddenly, during an awkward encounter they can keep a straight face, even say "sorry" and walk away thinking, how sad and nasty the person really was. Have fun rehearsing different scenarios for this little life saver at home!

C7: Control

In an ideal world, parents would patiently listen to the concerns of their children. Kids would always acknowledge the wishes of parents, and on the rare occasion an impasse occurred, then together they'd find a compromise. In our less than perfect world, parents who strive to give their child 'a voice' are far more likely to leave their child with a sense of dignity. When this happens, kids are inclined to make better choices and show flexible thinking. The best 'disaster recipe' is when we deliver quick ultimatums and back kids into a corner. Of course they'll lash out to self-protect!

In reality our world is filled with great kids who, from time to time, draw on 'power styled' tactics to help them feel more in control of situations. This primitive urge delivers a whopping adrenaline hit that convinces them they will get what they want and feel safer when they grab control. After all, they've used the tactic before - refusal, hiding, tantrums, screaming or hitting - and feel secure knowing how the script should play out for them!

When you find yourself dealing with your child's 'primitive control response' here are a few tips to improve the flexibility of their thinking, and your own;

1. All kids are reliant on composed adults. Stay calm and think whether this is worth pursuing or dodging.

2. Their behaviour happens for a reason. So, what's driving it this time? Got an easy circuit breaker to draw on?

3. Always have 'Plan B' in the back of your mind in case 'Plan A' turns out not so well.

4. Ask, "What can I do to help?" Kids often know what will work best. Remember, helping doesn't mean giving in.

5. Be compassionate. Even though you are the reason they aren't getting what they want, you can be sympathetic!

6. Do the unexpected. Humour, without sarcasm, can be wonderfully therapeutic for everyone.

7. A hug, a tussle of the hair, a kiss, a hi-5, and knuckles at the right moment can be wonderfully soothing. A warm NTH (Non Talking Hug) simply lets them know that you know they're doing it tough. Over time your children will see this as a vote of confidence in their capacity to manage.

8. If the issue is worth following through, say, "You're right I can't make you do something you don't want to do." State the consequence if they choose not to do it. State that you know they can make a good decision. Then get out of their way so they are not feeling the pressure of having to instantly reform.

9. When your child is highly emotional, make it a rule not to participate in problem solving at this moment. Wait (even if it is the next day), until their emotions are in check and they can think with a clear head. Let kids know that when we deliberately place ourselves in a calmer state our bodies receive a signal from our brains to relax. This in turn, switches on our ability to think! So the next time your child is faced with a wobbly moment, say, "We'll talk about it once you're feeling calmer. Cool brains make the best decisions". Sometimes they'll try to reduce their discomfort by winding you up. Do not accept the invitation into their emotional vortex. Simply say, "Hey, I love you way too much to argue about this." Then move away. Later, when they've regained their composure make yourself available and ask, "What do you think you can do about this?"

A catastrophe scale

Use a catastrophe scale. Graduate it from 1 to 5, with 1 being a 'slight setback' and 5 being a 'total disaster'. This provides a way for your child to rate the intensity of the problem before they respond. It helps them ask, "How big is this?" "Will it really matter later?" "Is it so bad that it has to wreck my day?" Many of us tend to catastrophise and initially think the problem is much worse than it is. Rating the problem helps to keep it in perspective.

5: a total disaster!

4: a worry

3: a trouble

2: an upset

1: slight setback

Make a poster

Make and display posters; Place them on a wall at home as a reminder for everyone. Here are a few positive phrases to help kids stay within the resilient thinking zone;

"I can do this. First, I need to…"
"When I stay calm I give my brain the best chance to think…"
"I can think of 2 ways to do this…"
"Before I do anything, I'll give it a rating on my catastrophe scale…"

C8: Communication

Communication is about listening to our kids, validating how they feel, and responding to promote their independent thinking. However, being an active listener isn't as easy as it sounds. You see, our instinctive urge is to rescue them from their heartache or discomfort by fixing problems for them as fast as possible! To be a clever active listener, simply rephrase back to them what they have just said, either as a statement validating their thoughts, or as a question for them to think on. Use a tone that sooths and offers dignity;

Tell me again, what did he say to you?
Wow, how did you feel?
I would have felt the same.
What did you say back?
How do you think he felt when you said that?
Do you think that made things better or worse?
So, what do you think he should do to make this better?
What can you do to help fix this?
How can I help you to do that?
(Be very clear as to how much you should buy into this)

This is a steadying approach for anyone wrestling with intense feelings. It sounds strange, but the objective isn't to fix your child's problem. It's more about helping them see that they can process complicated feelings and can work out solutions. Finally, when the right moment crops up, never shy away from sharing embarrassing stories about the times you handled a situation poorly - make it entertaining. It is therapeutic for children to learn that their mothers and fathers also experienced difficult times with their feelings when they were young.

C9: Competition

We live in a time where it is popular to have all children feeling as though they are winners and they can achieve anything. How misguided! There will always be winners and losers. We suggest that losing, when it is thoughtfully contrived, can be helpful to a child's emotional development. Through losing our children learn;

• none of us are fabulous at all things all of the time, and nor are we expected to be
• we lose because at that time we were not as lucky or as skilled as another, and that's life
• to appreciate the winner's talent or luck
• that the effort they have put in is also a great reward and can never be taken away
• how to re-group their emotions, bounce back and strive again
• how good it feels to honestly win or succeed
• to control feelings as they need to be gracious in the face of disappointment

Winning and losing? View it rationally, and see it as another way to enhance your child's emotional development - it's a part of the ebb and flow of life.

C10: Common sense

If your child is a worrier there are things worth thinking about. Firstly, genuine worries need to be listened to and be normalised. However, common sense tells us that worries are always best listened to in the light of daytime, rather than as the 'lights out' time approaches. Make it a rule to listen to your child's worries in the day time and place a time limit on these sorts of conversations. One approach is to have your child draw their worry on to a slip of paper. Then, they post it into their worry tin. It's just a matter of buying a small tin with a slot in the lid. For extra security so the worry won't escape you might get a tin with a tiny padlock on the lid. Once the worry has been discussed, written, folded up and slotted away into the tin, it doesn't need any further energy spent on it.

The fascinating part is that when the worries are looked at months later most children say, "That worry sounds silly now". This in itself delivers a healthy message about how much value we should give to worrying.

Common sense also tells us that being distressed or unhappy from time to time is normal. In practical terms, there is an art to supporting kids when they are upset. None of us like to see our children in pain, and our impetuous reaction might be to spend an excessive amount of time chatting about the issue with them. Occasionally this may be prudent, but if we tend to do this regularly, we teach them that a great way to get our undivided attention is for them to have yet 'another problem'. This creates an unsound pattern of thinking and can cause kids to dwell, and even obsess, on issues - making having problems the centre of their being. Counter-productive strategies as these actually prevent our children from setting up dependent patterns of recovery.

Chapter 10:
Navigating life's ups and downs

To finish up

Raising our children's emotional resilience is about 'guiding' their attitudes to deal more constructively with the ups and downs that life brings. To be honest, it's not a new program or another new-age therapist seen on morning television that will tip the balance. So much of raising resilient kids comes in the form of being a clever 'life-coach' who is prepared to gently and intelligently chip away. Isn't it ironic that their eventual resilience hinges on ours for the first twevnty years of their life?

My Notes:

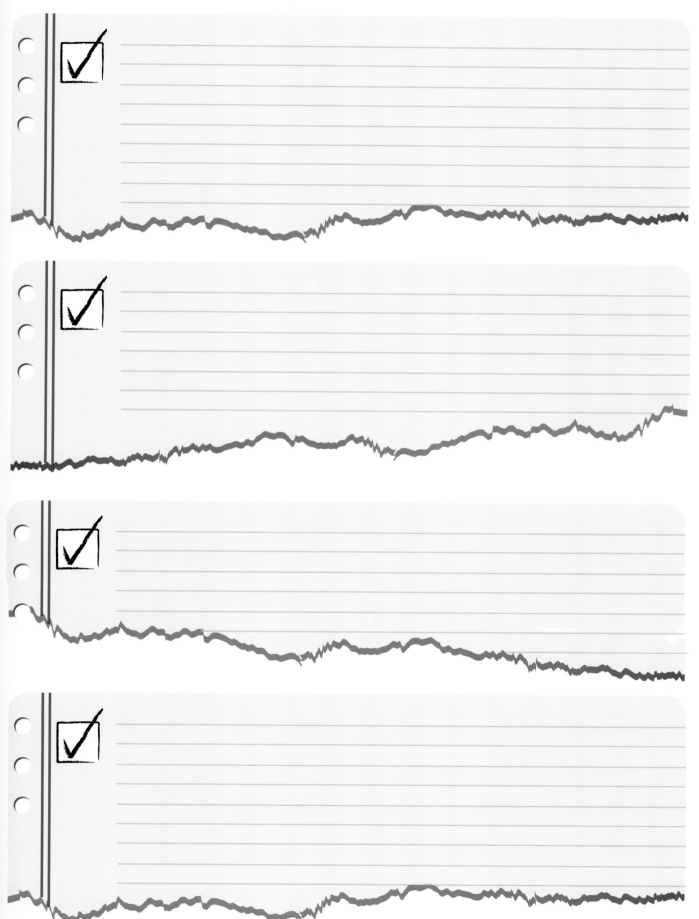

Recipe rescue:

ideas to organise your way through a better morning routine

The scenario...

Ingredients:

- **A disorganised parent**
- **Parents in conflict with one another**
- **Parents with inconsistent expectations**
- **Parents who don't know how-to set up structures to strengthen family organisation**
- **Parents not prepared to teach kids how-to follow, and stick with a schedule**
- **Parents who will not follow through with positive and negative consequences**
- **Parents who use this sorry circumstance as 'a badge of honour'-"Oh you think your kids are hard to get organised in the morning, you should see mine!"**
- **Kids actively seeking to control or oppose parents**
- **Kids with genuine organisational difficulties - children with poor memory and weak capacity to sustain concentration - for example, those with ADHD and mental health issues**
- **Kids who have unrestricted access to television or game consoles before school**

"What about my toast?"

It's just hit 8:05am and eleven year old Justin isn't ready to leave. He's only just pulled on his school pants. Despite the fact that everyone has to be in the car by 8:10am, he's in 'Justin's world', dawdling aimlessly about with one shoe in hand. Who knows where the other one is? Justin doesn't!

As usual, Justin's been slow to move even though everyone has places to be and the pressure to get ready is on. Gillian has been into his room six times - to get him out of bed, prize him away from sitting on his bed staring at the floor, to insist that he takes his pyjamas off, help him take his pyjamas off, to take away his iPod touch and later to turn off the television in his room. She'll never forgive herself for agreeing to have a TV in his room - her worst decision

ever and a decision that costs her every day!

"Justin, have you had breakfast or packed your schoolbag yet?"

Gillian instantly knows the answer to both questions as she spies his lunch box and breakfast still sitting on the kitchen counter with his homework book from last night.

"Justin, move it! Get your shoes on and pack your bag. You can eat a piece of toast in the car." Gillian throws a slice of bread into the toaster.

"I can't find my other shoe," whines Justin.

"Look under your bed," Gillian calls through gritted teeth.

Justin wanders toward his bedroom while Chelsea, his eight year old sister stands in the hallway, bag over her shoulder and ready to go.

Justin arrives back in the kitchen with both shoes. Thank goodness for small mercies Gillian thinks! She throws his lunchbox into his school bag, along with his homework book and heads for the door.

"What about my toast?" calls Justin. It's now 8:20am. The kids will be late for school, Gillian will be late for her team meeting and she's about ready to pop.

"Just get in the car! Both of you! Now!" she growls at the kids.

"Don't blame me for him being slow, Mum," says Chelsea as Gillian runs back into the house to retrieve the toast for Justin.

Organisation - first, identify the root of the difficulty

Where does your children's inept organisation stem from? Is it because you're disorganised and you've not taught them how to be organised? Is it due to their poor personal capacity or is it all about opposing you and trying to sabotage routines you try to put in place?

Some children and teens are genuinely organisationally challenged. It is a brain based difficulty where they really do have trouble remembering tasks, keeping focus - especially the ones we ask them to do - and completing everyday jobs. Parents often say, "they live in their own world" or "in a fog". Their lives are fractured by lost belongings, forgotten schoolwork, lost homework, poor planning, poor time-management and daily vagueness. Frequently, their untidy appearance or messy bedroom gives us a glimpse into their disorganised/ disordered thinking. While organisational challenges actually pervade most parts of their lives, the morning routine and its constraints on time, is when these invisible developmental flaws are most noticeable.

For some, memory and organisational weaknesses are linked to a specific learning difficulty. We know that children and teens diagnosed with ADD and ADHD suffer badly from time 'blindness' and poor task completion. In fact, they may be delayed by up to 40% compared to others the same age, despite average or well above average intelligence. Children with developmental immaturities, low motivation, auditory processing weaknesses, reduced listening capacities, and those experiencing depression, stress and anxiety can experience the same types of organisational deficits. Poorly organised kids lack the individual building blocks responsible for higher-order organisation. Without these primary components, they cannot look, feel or be well organised.

Does this help you form a better sense of the origin of your child's organisational problems? If so, you can see that independent organisation is a higher-order skill they haven't yet acquired, and the only way to support them is to gently and continuously coach them, as we set up consistent routines and structures.

Recipe rescue:

ideas to organise your way through a better morning routine

Are your school mornings chaotic? Are your mornings a high-nag, high-anxiety war zone? Are you tired of the machine gun bursts of frantic instructions that spray from your mouth, but never seem to have much of an impact?

"Hurry up, get out of bed", "Get dressed", "Go to the toilet", "Brush your teeth", "Find your shoes", "Put your shoes on", "Pack your bag", For God's sake just straighten your bed", "Put the milk back in the fridge", "That's too much cereal", "Why have you opened that juice?", "Pack your homework into your bag", "Nobody sits on the toilet for that long", while you scurry from location to location stamping out grass fires trying to get dressed and hang out a load of washing.

If some or all of this has a familiar ring to it, then this Recipe rescue is just what you need! It offers parents a blend of strategies that strike a balance between supporting kids and teens who have organisational difficulties, and those who have been allowed to fall into poor morning habits.

Chapter 11:

Navigating the Morning Madness

First, organise yourself!

Don't underestimate the high-stress around busy school mornings. School mornings have to be the most demanding time of the day because there's so much to do and a limited amount of time to do it. When we're in a rush and under pressure, we don't give clear directions to the kids. Instead, we bark out what needs to be done, and the tone is usually hurried, angry or condescending. The most important ingredient to low-stress mornings comes from organising yourself first!

The best tip - get out of bed well before the kids. Get showered, dressed and ready before you start the kids off for the morning. By doing this, you're free to actively work alongside your kids to help them develop and maintain the regular before school routine you wish to set in place. Smooth mornings don't just happen! They are engineered - the result of forward thinking and cleverly arranged conditions.

Bear in mind that our brains, and our kid's brains, take time to boot up after waking up - none of us have the same brainpower we're likely to generate later in the day. Adolescents get the worst of this. Current brain research shows that teen's brains aren't properly booted up until mid-morning because they experience forward shifts in their sleep

cycle by 1 to 2 hours. Apparently, the sleep-promoting hormone, melatonin, rises later in the day in teenagers than in kids and adults. That's why most teens will say that they're not tired, not ready to go to bed and can't fall asleep in the evening. Consequently, teens are programmed to stay up later, fall asleep

> *When we're in a rush and under pressure, we don't give clear directions to the kids. Instead, we bark out what needs to be done, and the tone is usually hurried, angry or condescending.*

later and sleep in longer. And, this is in its pure form - without the addictive influences of television, computers, video games or social media.
So given this, getting up earlier, and being a little more organised may be the very best strategy we have

available to us. We dare you to trial it! Come on! For one week, get yourself out of bed thirty minutes earlier and get yourself ready before it's time for the kids to stir. If you're not in a more settled state of mind and a step ahead of the kids we'll happily share eating this book! We know that we'll never risk eating our book because 'Murphy's Law' swings into action when you're behind the eight ball and pushed for time. When your planning puts you ahead of time, those few inevitable hiccups tend not to turn into cataclysmic disasters! Oh, and by the way, it models wonderful forward planning to the kids!

Checklists

Both of us, in our previous lives as teachers in classrooms, saw the dramatic difference between kids who've experienced chaotic mornings at home and those who've followed an anticipated before-school routine. The contrast is striking! And, for kids facing learning difficulties, anxiety issues, social hitches or behavioural turbulence, the contrast is even starker. Children and young teens who arrive at school following typical morning mayhem can take most of the morning to come down from a high arousal state - hyperactive/ hypervigilant - to a place where they can begin to engage in learning and with peers. Add an empty stomach to this because they chose television or video games over eating breakfast, and the morning becomes even more problematic.

Morning checklists are such a simple thing to do. The appeal is that they break tasks down into smaller, more manageable steps. They bring guaranteed predictability to mornings, especially if you've encouraged your kids to take part in their design. Yes, allow them to take some control because having a sense of control usually adds to their investment to make it work.
A checklist doesn't take long to make. You can make them on your computer or they can be bought from stationery

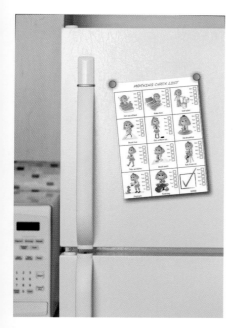

retailers. Because of their flexibility - using word or picture prompts - they can be designed for both young and older children. A further option is to take photos of what the completed morning task looks like using your smartphone and import the photo into the checklist. If you aren't sure how to do this, there's a good chance one of the kids will be delighted to show you! To help you get off to a quick start we've designed a picture-prompt and word-styled morning checklist at the end of the chapter. Feel free to photocopy them, or go to our websites to download the pdfs; www.marklemessurier.com.au (Mark) and www.hansberryec.com.au (Bill). Once you've done this, laminate the checklist and have your children use non-permanent marker or stickers that can be removed each week. By doing this, the checklist can be reused week after week.

Always display the checklist where it is most likely to capture your children's attention and trigger their memory. Most kids get a kick from the act of ticking a task off or placing a sticker on it as they move through the list. The act of ticking off a completed task is actually motivating. For the kids who are harder to motivate, a selection of treats - nuts, a zany lucky dip, smarties, money, phone credit and so on - placed near the checklist as they tick

the chart always adds enthusiasm! If you are very organised yourself and have your jobs done, you could station yourself close to the checklist and dispense the motivational goodies as the kids swing by to tick a job off! Oh, be sure to take it down when friends or extended family come over. Always safeguard your children's dignity! Also, don't forget Chorepad. It's a clever little Token Reinforcement App for iPhones and iPads that we mentioned in the chapter, *How-to catch and build positive behaviours*. It's a wonderful way to keep track of before and after school chores and keeps kids interested!

How-to make a morning routine

Timing is the key. Choose a time when the pressure is off. Family meetings work well for this type of planning. Otherwise, go for a lazy Sunday morning when no one has anywhere to be. Sit down as a family and talk about the things that need to get done to make school mornings easier. Chat with the kids about what happens when mornings work well and what happens when mornings get tough and stressful. Be sure to mention that you want to create mornings that work well! As you all chat, jot down the morning tasks that the kids mention. Avoid the temptation to add too many! A list of more than five tasks is too big for most kids, so stick to the basics and assign a digital time for each;

- Time to get out of bed on time
- Time to get dressed
- Time to eat breakfast
- Time to finish breakfast, place dishes on sink and get the lunchbox packed
- Time to get the schoolbag packed
- Time to be walking out the door for school

Think about it - if school mornings are currently a struggle in your home, how much easier might it be if your kids started doing just two of these tasks more consistently? It would have to make a difference. Remember, you're not looking for immediate miraculous transformations, just steady improvement.

When you see one of the kids looking lost or distracted, say, "Check your list. Where are you up to?" Resist telling them what isn't done - praise them for what they have done - remember that you are promoting patterns of independence. You are in coaching mode, and it will take a while. The end game is making your involvement redundant!

Screens, free-time and the morning schedule

We subscribe to the idea that the faster the morning tasks are done, the longer the free-time the kids have available to them. So when you're planning the new morning routine ask the kids what they'd like to do when they finish up early. Create an ingenious list, and then display it so they can draw from it to reward themselves.

In our opinion, allowing children to access screens as they get ready in the morning is a dire mistake. Most kids are not able to self-regulate what they do when they have a screen in front of their face, or a controller in their hands - it's natural for them to be totally absorbed by the screen. What you'll get is your child in ultra-slow motion, with their school shirt half buttoned, one shoe on (no sock) and eyes frozen on the screen, as if in a trance, even in the coldest of weather.

If you're adamant that screens must be part of free-time, then we suggest you put them last on the list of morning tasks. Let access to them be an incentive for completing morning tasks. We know some very clever parents who do just this, but the screens are not used at home. Instead, they hand the screens to their children to use in the car as they travel to school. Oh, if one of the kids turns a screen on while your back is turned, play it calmly and take possession of the device. Don't go on and on about it, simply gather up remotes and important connecting cords with the understanding that they will be handed over when you choose.

A great morning routine starts with a good afternoon routine

Lots of morning hot spots can be eliminated by developing a planned afternoon routine which swings into action the moment the kids arrive home. Helping your children to embed some simple habits will save precious time the next morning:

– *Taking lunch boxes and school newsletters out of the schoolbag and putting them in an assigned place Putting schoolbags in an agreed spot*

– *Taking the school uniform off and putting it in the dirty clothes basket or hanging it ready for the next day*

– *Putting the school shoes in the same place*

– *Setting homework up and doing it in the usual spot Putting books, pencil cases back into the schoolbag after homework is finished and the school diary is signed*

– *Eating dinner with the family at the same time most nights*

– *Having a shower or bath at the usual time – much better to get this out the way in the evening!*

– *Slipping into bed at the same time each night so your child is getting their required 9.5 hours of sleep*

Why not make a checklist to establish the after school tasks your children need to do?

Schoolbags

A messy schoolbag undermines any well-planned routine. We've all experienced a moment of panic as we discover something of consequence from school that should have been taken care of last week! It's challenging

for most kids to keep schoolbags well organised and tenfold harder for those with organisational and attentional difficulties. There's a simple rule here - never allow schoolbag untidiness to become an issue. Instead, once a week go through the school bag with your child. Sure, set it up so they take the leading role, and no doubt you'll both be amazed by what you discover; notes, newsletters, library books, lunch bags, toys, collector cards and food that has accumulated at the bottom of the bag. But, beyond this is the development of a practical habit and the feeling that they can begin the new week knowing exactly what's in the bag.

Finally, if you think this approach is only suitable for young children, you couldn't be more wrong. This is an approach we consistently use in our work with motivated, but disorganised students in the upper years of high school. Carried out with respect, it works beautifully!

Are you a 'homework rescuer'?

Stop it! You're not doing any of your kids a favour - in fact, you're damaging their organisational difficulty. Your actions may be inspired by love, but what you're doing is misguided. Sit down with the kids and tell them that you will no longer be available for homework rescue at the eleventh hour, in the mornings or evenings. Explain that from now on if they have unfinished homework, they can wake up early and use their free-time to do it, but you will not be available to help. In contrast, make it perfectly clear that you'll always be available to support homework when it's part of a longer-term planned, organised approach. Whatever their age, now is the time to let them live with the consequences of unfinished homework, and failure to listen and follow basic requests. For some of you who will have an uphill battle ahead, we suggest that you let your child's teacher know you've made this the policy at home. Most teachers will appreciate this. Some will even open up and let students complete their homework before classes begin in the morning, but don't necessarily expect this.

Eating breakfast

As parents, we're constantly hammered by the media, faddy food gurus, breakfast food companies and our kids about what's best for breakfast. Sadly, many of kids' top choices are nutritionally poor and loaded with staggering amounts of sugar, fat, preservatives and colourings. What you decide to feed your kids is outside the scope of this book, but one thing is for sure - what you feed them will influence their mood, concentration, cooperation, social responsiveness, enthusiasm, memory, desire to follow instructions, learning capacities, and will gradually impact on their future.

Pancakes, toast, croissants, fruit juices and many cereals and mueslis are not ideal breakfast foods, but something is a bit better than nothing. Nutritious sources of breakfast protein include milk, cheese, yoghurt, baked beans, soy products, nuts, white meat and eggs. Other good choices include whole grains and fruits. The experts tell us that by mixing these foods, the body is fuelled for longer because blood sugar levels remain higher for much longer. These foods are said to have a low G.I. index.

If your child baulks at eating breakfast, try not to turn your worry into a battle. This rubs against the principle of assisting kids to be more responsible for their choices. Negotiate something they will eat and drink, even if it is in small quantities, and pack extra food in their lunch box for them to nibble later. Take them shopping to choose breakfasts that are acceptable to both of you. Having chosen their breakfast foods themselves may help strengthen their promise to eat in the morning and make breakfasts a little easier.

It may seem a little extreme, but consider getting the kids to set their place at the table the night before. It's a great idea because psychologically it cues children into a predictable start. They know exactly what they are going to eat and drink for breakfast, and have it ready to go.

And, as tough is it may sound, kids of all ages do better at the breakfast table when a parent is nearby or sitting with them. It's just a fact of life!

Cueing systems to go!

Countdown till leaving time

"The car leaves in 30 minutes", "The car leaves in 20 minutes", "The car leaves in 10 minutes" "The car leaves in 5 minutes" Get the idea? Kids don't perceive the passing of time as we do, and because we're often battling to make time we view it with way more reverence than our kids do. Add to the picture any type of attentional difficulty, processing issue or memory weakness a child has, and tracking time gets even trickier. With younger kids, give them five minute time calls. Then, as they become familiar with how time passes, work your calls out to ten minute intervals. This is great training and also gets the kids into the habit of clock watching.

Chapter 11:

Navigating the Morning Madness

Timers of all sorts

Get visual! Use whiteboard markers on the glass over the clock face in the kitchen. Create coloured regions by shading them in - green for 40-20 minutes left before departure, orange for 20-10 minutes left and red for the final 10 minutes.

Any of the kid's 'idevices'- iPods, iPads or smartphones - have countdown timer features. Set it at one hour before the leave time. Just by keeping an eye on it, or listening to it, their performance is likely to be improved!

Another creative option is to use a *sand timer* (*www.youtube.com/watch?v=eIrwDFU6GTg* and *www.youtube.com/watch?v=PpxeWiu3zC8*) or a *goo timer* (*www.youtube.com/watch?v=FzFosq94WOk* and *www.youtube.com/watch?v=rfiXKdMdbpk*) as a visual reminder of time passing. They're portable and can be displayed as your kids tackle homework, have a shower, get dressed in the morning, run an errand, pick up the doggy-poo, or wait to use the computer or television. Timers, including the cheapest of stop watches, are persuasive visual reminders about the progression of time and can be an incentive to stick with a task for just a little longer.

Piggyback

Piggybacking is an engaging strategy to help memory and it's so simple! Bring together something your child usually forgets with something that they regularly enjoy as part of their day. If, for example, your child has no

difficulty remembering to pour themselves a bowl of their favourite breakfast cereal, but has trouble putting their used bowl into the dishwasher, try placing a bright sticky note with a reminder "used dishes go in the…" on the cereal box. Piggyback combinations are infinite and can be fun and motivating for kids.

Create a play list

A few of our musically inspired parents, who perhaps secretly hold DJ'ing aspirations, have made a one-hour playlist of songs and play them each morning for all to hear. The first song - the wake up song, right through to the

last song, which begins 3 minutes before everyone has to be out the door! Twelve to fifteen songs take approximate an hour to play. This brilliant auditory cueing approach works a treat as kids quickly associate certain songs with the remaining time left and learn to pace themselves to the music.

Set the deadline and be faithful to your word

Each of the cuing systems described hinge on parents setting a deadline and sticking to it! Once you've set up the system with the kids, give them a week's grace to get used to it. Following the week's trial, it starts in earnest! Explain that those who choose not to be ready on time will face the following:

Those still in their pyjamas will leave the house and go to school in their pyjamas.
In the rare instance you need to apply this keep your resolve. Yes, there will be tears! Deal with this graciously by handing your child their school clothes

as you bustle them out of the door so they can hurriedly get dressed in the car on the way to school.

Bags not properly packed will go as they are.
It's too late! So, if homework, a book, a musical instrument or sports clothes didn't make it to the bag, your child will need to deal with the consequence at school.

Lunch boxes not packed into bags will not be rescued from the fridge or kitchen bench.
You may wish to keep a box of very plain muesli bars in the car to ensure they have something to nibble, but let's be honest - they won't starve!

Deciding on negative consequences for persistent forgetfulness and disorganisation involves walking a fine line. On one hand, we have an appreciation that some of our kids find organisation truly elusive and that it may be part of an impairment. Yet, if we constantly allow them to ignore sensible structures put in place without a negative consequence, then we provide them with no motivation to improve. So, providing well-developed structures are in place, it is highly appropriate for a negative consequence to be consistently applied when they fail to meet a reasonable expectation.

Consequences may include the loss of a favourite television program or screens, early to bed, completing extra chores, and so on during the following afternoon or evening. Let the consequences do the talking - for most of us, personal inconvenience usually increases our desire to do better!

Let your optimism take control

" I can see you've already checked a few off. Well done!"

" Wow, you're on a mission this morning!"

" Someone's headed for free time!"

" What a delight it is to watch you organise yourself"

" Boy our house runs well in the morning when you do that!"

" Careful, you'll set the morning checklist on fire if you keep ticking jobs off that fast!"

Remember to incorporate positive words and an encouraging spirit. Even as you spy one of the kids dawdling, use language that highlights your trust in them.

Celebrate Success

Make a deal with the kids that five successful mornings in a row wins a family outing to a movie or favourite restaurant! If this is too much for them to achieve, then make the goal just three successful mornings in a row!

This is an ideal way to kick start things, then progressively build the rewards out and gradually fade them away.

If you believe that a child is likely to struggle with the new schedule then consider two things. Firstly, review just how realistic your expectations are. Should you simplify the schedule to reduce demands on them and ensure a better chance of success? Secondly, don't make it so they have to achieve a particular number of successful mornings in a row. Instead, agree on a number together, and even if it takes a while celebrate when they achieve success!

MORNING CHECK LIST

Mon ☐ Tues ☐ Wed ☐ Thur ☐ Fri ☐ **Get out of bed**	Mon ☐ Tues ☐ Wed ☐ Thur ☐ Fri ☐ **Make bed**	Mon ☐ Tues ☐ Wed ☐ Thur ☐ Fri ☐ **Use toilet**
Mon ☐ Tues ☐ Wed ☐ Thur ☐ Fri ☐ **Brush hair**	Mon ☐ Tues ☐ Wed ☐ Thur ☐ Fri ☐ **Get uniform on**	Mon ☐ Tues ☐ Wed ☐ Thur ☐ Fri ☐ **Eat breakfast**
Mon ☐ Tues ☐ Wed ☐ Thur ☐ Fri ☐ **Tidy up dishes**	Mon ☐ Tues ☐ Wed ☐ Thur ☐ Fri ☐ **Brush teeth**	Mon ☐ Tues ☐ Wed ☐ Thur ☐ Fri ☐ **Get shoes on**
Mon ☐ Tues ☐ Wed ☐ Thur ☐ Fri ☐ **Feed pet**	Mon ☐ Tues ☐ Wed ☐ Thur ☐ Fri ☐ **Pack bag**	Mon ☐ Tues ☐ Wed ☐ Thur ☐ Fri ☐ **DONE!**

My Notes:

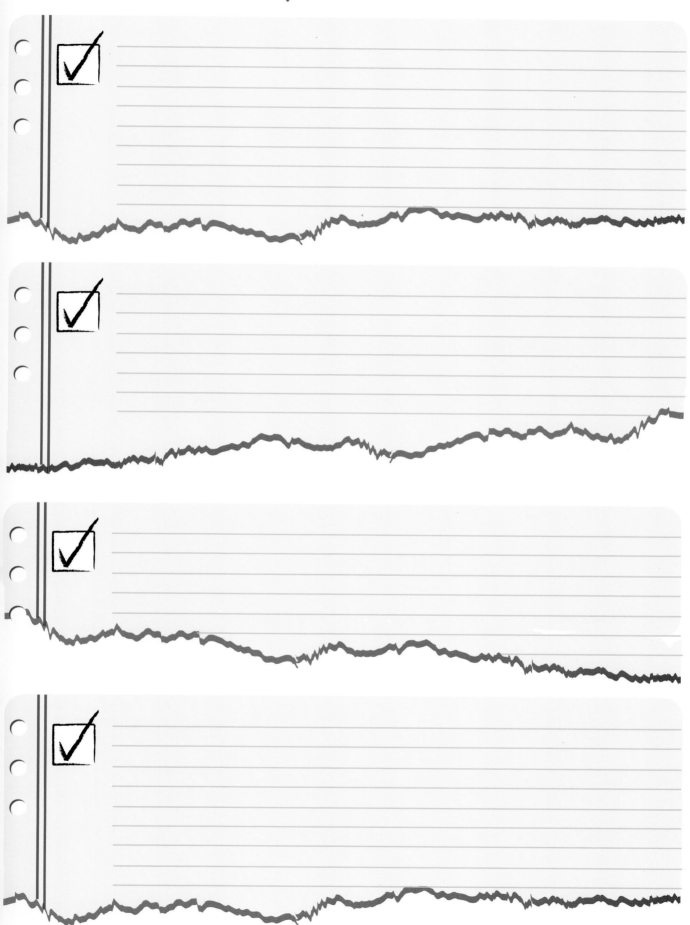

Chapter 12:
Chores, pocket money and saving

Recipe rescue:

teaching kids to belong by contributing

Ingredients:

- **Parents who never had to help around the home as kids, so don't have the experience**
- **Parents who do not understand the benefits kids feel by contributing**
- **Kids who've been parented to believe that they are entitled and are not required to help**
- **Kids who will not reach out to make the lives of their family a bit easier**
- **A mother or father who are completely in the service of their kids**
- **Parents who are too busy to put in the work required to teach their kids how-to contribute**

The scenarios...

Ella's gets grounded again

"Ella, for the third time, get off your phone and tidy up the mess you've left in the bathroom. Your wet towel has been on the floor and the hair straighter in the basin all day. Move them!"

Fourteen year old Ella rolls her eyes and complains into the phone to her friend, "Hold on a minute. Mum wants me to be her slave again."

Enraged, Leanne's eyes widen. "What did you just say?"
She snatches the phone from Ella and terminates the conversation.

"You've no right to do that!" roars Ella.

"Oh, like the way you have no right to leave the bathroom in a mess.

You left your hair straightener on. You could've burnt the house down," bites Leanne.

"That's why I left it in the basin ... dah! At least I know that porcelain won't catch fire. Where did you go to school?"

"So you knew you left it on?" screams Leanne aghast.

"Yeah," scoffs Ella.

"What planet do you come from?" shouts Leanne. "Since when do we leave electrical appliances running all day?"

"Well, I would've had time to turn it off if you weren't yelling at me like a nut case to get in the car this morning," taunts Ella.

"That's it Ella, you're totally grounded for a month." Ella gasps, but Leanne is just revving up. "You do nothing around the house but make mess for others to clean up. I have to nag to get you to do anything. You treat this place like it's a hotel and we're your staff. You do nothing to help here, Ella, nothing, and I'm completely over it. Until you start to show some cooperation and contribute to the house, there'll be no allowance, no sport, no friends' houses, no parties, no screens and no mobile phone."

Leanne believes she's delivered the knock-out punch.

"What?" blubbers Ella.

"You heard, Ella. Until we see some contribution from you, your world will be very small and very lonely."

I want and I get

"Mum, I want this App for my IPod. It's just $2.99. It's a really good game. Everyone at school has it," asks eleven year old Riley enthusiastically.

"What happened to the ten dollars I gave you on Tuesday? I asked you to put some of that aside for times like this," protests Sandra. "What on earth did you spend it on?"

"I, er… I didn't spend it. I think I lost it at school" Riley hesitantly responds.

Sandra feels her breathing quicken. "Why did you take the money to school?" The fuse has been lit and Sandra is ready to explode. "You know that I don't want you taking money to school unless it's for the tuck shop! When are you going to learn that money doesn't grow on trees? Your father and I go to work to earn that money and you spend it as though there's an endless supply of it. You have no idea of the value of money. That's it! That's the last dollar you'll get from me."

The next day at soccer, Riley runs up to Sandra with his two friends Josh and Callum in tow. All the boys have their iPods in hand. "Mum, can I download a game to your phone? Callum and Josh both have it". Sandra, deep in conversation with a friend, hands Riley her phone, "Here, stop interrupting." Sandra replies as she momentarily breaks from her conversation. Thirty seconds later, the new $2.99 App is downloaded. Riley's timing and persistence has paid off!

What's fair?

Jan and Peter have two sons. There's easy going, thirteen year old Jack, who's usually cooperative and contributes to chores around the house. Then, there's Clancy! He's eleven years old and does nothing around the house unless nagged and closely supervised. Without supervision it's typical to find the canned dog food uncovered inside the fridge with a spoon still inside it, or a trail of garbage down the hallway that's escaped from the plastic bin liner as he's dragged it to the wheelie bin.

Over time, the gap between the boys' contribution to chores has widened and resentment towards Clancy has built. So, Jan and Peter decide to make it fairer. They announce that pocket money earned from chores will be the boys' spending money on an up-coming family holiday, hoping this will be an incentive for Clancy to show greater responsibility.

"Why is Clancy going to get the same pocket money as me when you always remind him and do it with him?" protests Jack. "Anyway, you'll just keep paying him whether he does the jobs or not. It's what you've always done. It's not fair!" Jan and Peter see Jack's point. It makes them think. Have they made a reasonable decision? Is their decision loaded for or against Clancy? Are they disadvantaging Jack? Are they honestly prepared to make Clancy miss out on things that Jack will be able to afford on the holiday? Is this in the spirit of a great family holiday?

Are any of these scenarios slightly familiar?

In the first scenario, fourteen year old Ella's spectacular lack of care and cooperation has driven her mum to 'Armageddon styled' consequences. In the second, eleven year old Riley's lack of respect for money, and his persistence to extract it from his parents, have them worried. In the final scenario, Jan and Peter are on the cusp of a revolt in their home, as a chore-based pocket money system causes a gaping inequity. These parents, just as many of us do, are grappling with the big questions:

Should kids have regular chores?
Is it better to ask for help when a job needs doing?
Is it a good idea to pay the kids for chores so they can begin to control their own money?
Should money be given freely as the children's share of the family income?
How can pocket money be used to help kids become financially literate?

Chapter 12:

Chores, pocket money and saving

Recipe rescue:

teaching kids to belong by contributing

Your child's mental health depends on contribution

Let's hit the number one issue on the head. Kids must contribute! The level at which they pitch in must correspond to their age and capabilities. Equally, you must be wise about how you go about it. Basically, you have two choices. You can nag, browbeat and threaten the kids into doing chores, or you can progressively teach them how-to do chores, so it is seen as a way to naturally support one another.

Your parents may have once said, "You do the chores to help earn your keep." They knew what child wellbeing experts have been able to measure for some time. It is, kids who learn that they belong through their contributions, end up far healthier than those who are not required to pitch in at home. Emmy Werner's research on resilience found that the most resilient children

have been required to carry out socially desirable tasks - chores - to prevent others in their family or community from experiencing overload, distress or discomfort (Werner, 1984). Such acts, called 'required helpfulness', are proven to lead to lasting and positive emotional changes in the young helpers. Similarly, eastern philosophies persistently raise the notion that happiness comes from service to others. Most kids, however, do not spontaneously embrace a spirit of helpfulness around the home, or to others. This needs to be learned, and takes clever modeling and management by parents. Children need to be shown the way. They need to be taught how-to contribute with grace.

Start simply and start early. As soon as you feel each of your kids can contribute teach them when and how-to keep a space tidy, unpack their school bag, water a plant, place their dishes into

the sink, sweep a path, unpack the dishwasher, vacuum their room, rake leaves, straighten their bed and so on. A word of caution - whatever they do will never measure up to your standards! Don't believe us? Well, what about the cleaner who's paid to clean your home or office? How many conversations have you had with friends about the shortfall in their standards compared to your expectations? Why is it that we are often more tolerant towards those outside of our family?

...Most kids, however, do not spontaneously embrace a spirit of helpfulness around the home, or to others. This needs to be learned...

Let's get practical

How often have you thought, 'Heavens, getting her to do this darn job is actually making more work for me?' If you have, you're not alone. Teaching the kids to contribute around the house is 80% teaching and 20% about lightening your domestic load. For the lucky ones, the odds gradually fall in their favour over time. So, resist the urge to say - "Oh just give it to me. I may as well do it myself." Stick with coaching them, even if it means breaking tasks up into smaller, more doable chunks.

Match the task to the child

The golden rule is to match the chore to your child's skills and ability. So, start young children with the simplest of tasks. Select jobs they can do, will enjoy and gain a sense of satisfaction from. The end-game is to make sure they experience a sense of pride from being able to help out. This is the strongest motivator for contributions in the future.

A picture tells a thousand words!

Before you get the kids to attempt a job on their own, do it with them! Once it's done take some photos of what the completed job looks like. By doing this, your child can compare their attempts with what's expected. If you're iPod or smartphone savvy, dedicate a folder to images of 'jobs done well' - a clean room, a straightened bed, a tidy desk, a well raked lawn and more! When the kids come to you too quickly and say, "I've done it!" be ready to say, "Okay, let's get the photo so we can see how you've done." Get them to compare the picture with their effort and if there's more to be done, kindly point out what's still to do. In the early stages help them complete the task as part of the coaching process.

Remember that family mission statement?

Make sure the family mission statement - refer to the chapter on 'Rules' - includes an explicit statement about how the family takes care of one another by sharing jobs. It might include;

We share the jobs
We each help to keep a clean home
We all help to clean up

This clarifies that jobs aren't just for the adults - everyone contributes.

Start speaking 'contribution-ese'

Always thank the kids when they finish a chore and have shown care. After all, we appreciate being thanked for jobs we've done. We call this sort of feedback, 'contribution-ese' as it helps to ensure future contributions.

'Contribution-ese' focuses on contribution and how it makes life better for everyone. The crucial message - you belong in the world through your helpful contributions and interactions with one another.

Here are a few examples of 'contribution-ese';

- It makes it easier when the dishwasher is unpacked, thanks for that.
- The yard is such a nice place to be when it's raked. Was that you?
- It really helps everyone when the playroom is kept tidy - thanks.
- I was so pleased to see the living room vacuumed today. You've made everyone's day brighter!
- You've saved me an hour's work today by helping tidy the garage - that makes my day easier.
- It always puts me in a great mood when your room is tidy!
- I got such a pleasant surprise to come home and find the dishes done. Thanks for that.
- That's a job well done. Thanks for making things easier for everyone.

Chapter 12:

Chores, pocket money and saving

You scratch my back and I'll scratch yours!

Well, this is how life in the big wide world works. Remember, early in the chapter? That fracas between fourteen year old Ella and her mother, Leanne? Yes, Ella's adolescent brain was operating on an entirely different plane. In the Twilight Zone!

So, what's to be done when kids, younger and older, lose motivation to contribute to the household tasks? Here's an approach to teach an 'out of whack' teen potent lessons about how the world works, but it comes with some cautions;

Caution 1: *You should not enjoy this. If you receive pleasure from it, then your intent is revengeful rather than consequential - that's unhealthy.*
Caution 2: *Use a quiet, low emotional tone. Pick the right moment when you and your child are calm. Say what you need to say in as few words as possible, and then move away.*
Caution 3: *Once you've said what you need to say, expect your child to be annoyed and vent frustration. Do not buy into it.*

Now that you have the cautions, here's the plan. Find a time to sit down with your child, and together, generate a list of the things you do for them that make their lives more enjoyable, but please, stay away from being a martyr. Lists include:

- *Driving them to friends' houses*
- *Driving them to sport*
- *Driving them to parties or social outings*
- *Allowing them to use your television or computer*
- *Preparing their favorite meals*
- *Having their friends over in your home*
- *Having their friends for sleepovers*
- *Doing their washing*
- *Doing their ironing*
- *Paying their phone account*
- *Lending them the car*

When you think about it, there are many, many special things we do for our kids that add to their quality of life, and we would not suddenly be labelled 'neglectful' or 'punitive' if we decided to thoughtfully withdraw one or two of them from time to time. It's easy to lose sight of the difference between doing **'favours'** for the kids, and the things that they really are **'entitled to'**. So, once the list is completed, let them know that from now on you will work on the; you scratch my back and I'll scratch yours principle. This means that you will happily continue doing the extra things for them while they are 'pitching in' and doing their share around the house. However, you will withdraw doing some things, usually available to them, when they become uncooperative or indifferent.

So, how might this look? Here's an example;

"Clancy, you know how we've planned to have Josh for a sleepover on Friday night? Well, that depends on you getting the leaves on the back lawn raked and put into the super sack by dinner time today."

Notice the language? It's not hostile or threatening, but delivered with composure. And because of this, eleven year old Clancy is more likely to do the job willingly because his dignity remains intact. Let's move to the next step. There will be times you have to follow through with a consequence. Believe it or not, you can be sympathetic as you call off the sleepover by saying something like;

"I know how you feel, Clancy. It's a pain having to live with the consequences of your actions, isn't it? You're smart. You'll make a better choice next time."

Keep right away from, "You'll thank me for this one day!" Typically, the response will disappoint you, and so it should! No matter how you deliver the consequence, be prepared to be called "mean", "nasty", "unfair", "a loser", "embarrassing", "cruel", or "hate-worthy". Your job as an adult is to see their jibes as impotent. Don't respond. Good parenting has moments when it feels hard and appears thankless.

Spoilt kids always sabotage contribution

All kids need to know that they are unconditionally loved by their parents, but that's different to, "You are special just because you are you". This style of communication grows an unrealistic sense of 'entitlement' in children, leaving them with a confused view of their place in the world. The result is that these 'little princes' or 'little princesses' look and act spoilt. Their self-absorbed behaviour becomes seriously at odds with helping out around the house, or in fact putting themselves out to help anyone. When questioned about 'pitching in', they will tell you that they won't be treated as a slave, and when you say that if they don't 'pitch in' you're feeling like the slave, they'll roll their eyes, shrug and walk away.

As you well know, there are many miserable adults struggling to reconcile their distorted view of their place in the world due to a childhood of being indulged, doted on and believing they are entitled. Be careful about the seeds you sow.

The following 'reality styled tips for teenagers' has long been doing the e-mail rounds. Often, they're falsely attributed to Bill Gates, and if you can get past the hard edge, the list conveys the view that a sense of entitlement is unhealthy for young people.

RULES:

Rule 1: Life is not fair - get used to it!

Rule 2: The world doesn't care about your self-esteem. The world will expect you to accomplish something before you feel good about yourself.

Rule 3: You will not make $100,000 a year straight out of high school. You won't be a manager with a car, a car phone and bonuses until you earn them.

Rule 4: If you think your teacher is tough, wait till you get a boss.

Rule 5: Working in a fast food joint is not beneath your dignity. Your grandparents had a different word for this - "opportunity".

Rule 6: If you mess up, it's not your parents' fault - just learn from your mistake.

Rule 7: Before you were born, your parents were not as boring as they are now. They got that way from paying your bills, cleaning your clothes and listening to you talk about how cool you are. So before you save the rainforests, try delousing the cupboard in your own room.

Rule 8: Your school may have done away with winners and losers, but life has not. In some schools they'll give you as many times as you want to get the right answer. This doesn't have the slightest resemblance to anything in real life.

Rule 9: Life is not divided into semesters. You don't get summers off and very few employers are interested in helping you find yourself. You do that on your own time.

Rule 10: Television is not real life. In real life people have to leave the coffee shop and work.

Rule 11: Be nice to nerds. Chances are you'll end up working for one.

Is it wise to attach pocket-money to chores?

Now we've established that it's good for your kid's long-term mental health to contribute around the house, let's introduce the idea of pocket money. Some families instantly attach pocket money to household chores. They believe this will make their kids more diligent as well as teach them a bit about the 'hard knocks' of employment. This works well for a few kids, especially those like Jack in our second scenario. If you decide that your kids are similar to Jack and that you're clever enough to make it work, then here's a 'rule of thumb' we've discovered from our surveying. It is to award $0.20 per year of the child's age, per chore. This translates to a ten year old earning $12 a week for pocket money because they successfully complete six set chores each week.

Chapter 12:
Chores, pocket money and saving

Alternatively, you might wish to run a chore incentive styled system, take a look at the chapter called, How-to catch and build positive behaviours. It's filled with lots of appealing ways to implement these kinds of ideas.

Tyler used a chore incentive system

Twelve year old Tyler and his mum devised a clever point system which inspired him to contribute more around the house. Left to his own devices, he wouldn't do much. Under the new system he could earn a point for feeding the dog, two points for stacking the dishwasher, one point for making his bed and two points for taking out the recyclables each day. If Tyler completed his chores during the week, he was able to achieve 30 points. Dianne, his mum, and Tyler decided on a formula to convert points to dollars, and once every three or four weeks would buy something that he could not otherwise have. His first two purchases were two hard covered Star Wars Collector's editions, which he adored. Diane was clever. Prior to the system beginning she deliberately whetted Tyler's Star War appetite with a brief visit to the bookstore, a chance for him to hold the books, to flick pages and smell the new ink. That set the scene for a successful outcome! In the ensuing weeks, Dianne was happy to prompt Tyler, but the beauty of their simple system was the way it dramatically reduced his forgetfulness. It required little effort to maintain, as largely Tyler could be left to record the points on the tracking sheet taped to the fridge. It was a win/win solution!

When pocket money results in little or no improvement with chores, parents often lock themselves into a damaging power struggle with their kids. Be careful - avoid walking headlong into this obvious trap! Our preference is that kids should receive an allowance. This needs to be viewed as an automatic share of the family's income. The amount of money kids receive increases as they mature, and takes into account that teens will be using their allowance to fund more expensive pursuits, clothing and so on.

Moneyboxes, saving and banking

Typically, after a child first receives pocket money or an allowance you're likely to find it on the floor of their bedroom or in with the Lego. Don't despair, because when we view it through a young child's eyes it's easy to understand this. Even though they've worked for it, and looked forward to receiving it, they may have never used it. Think about it - in today's electronic world, kids don't often see money exchanged because wages are often paid directly to bank accounts, bills are paid online, goods are purchased by waving a plastic card past a beeping sensor and cash comes out of a hole in the wall. Given this, it's pretty hard for kids to conceptualize its actual worth in the beginning.

Get kids in to the habit of dividing their income

A sensible starting point is to pay young kids their pocket money or allowance in coins and help them to divide their income into what will be saved, spent and shared with charity.

Look over websites dedicated to teaching kids financial literacy and you'll find a recurring theme - the importance of teaching kids to save, spend and share. This simple formula suggests putting part of their pocket money or allowance aside to save, dedicating a part to give to charity and keeping part to spend.

Talk to anyone who has studied wealth creation and they'll mention George Clason's classic 'The Richest Man in Babylon' or 'Think and Grow Rich' by Napoleon Hill. They teach how-to develop good money habits, and the ideas and themes are still relevant today.

A number of families we work with use 'Moonjar' *(www.moonjar.com.au)*. This is a three-part moneybox with sections dedicated to saving, spending and sharing. It comes with a booklet containing ideas to teach financial literacy to kids. 'Moonjar' also has a passbook where kids can nominate the different percentages that will be

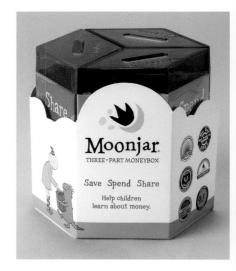

saved, spent and shared and record their deposits and withdrawals. Coupled with a child's savings bank account, this is a useful tool for teaching kids how to successfully navigate their financial future.

My Notes:

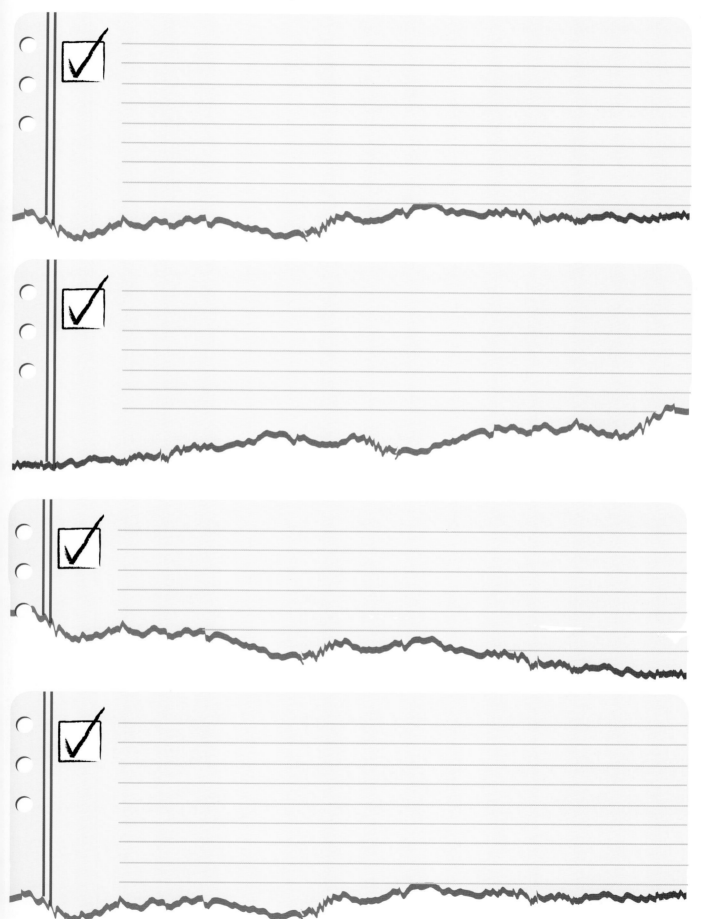

Chapter 13:
Mealtime mayhem

Recipe rescue:

ideas to improve mealtime connections

Ingredients:

- **A child fast learning how to use food to control parents**
- **A child who enjoys this battle**
- **A child learning to get attention for all the wrong reasons**
- **A child who may not be hungry, is weary or wants to get away from the table**
- **Parents who can't work out whether their child's reaction is about the food or about a battle with them**
- **A parent who freely battles over food**
- **A parent without a plan**
- **A parent resolute to make their child eat, or finish their plate**
- **An anxious parent worried that their child may go hungry**

The scenarios...

Discord
Dinner incites a division not seen in other parts of our family life!

"This smells funny", screwed up noses, "I didn't want this much". Then Michael, our five year old, starts up too. He quietly drops off his chair and disappears under the table. That fires me up, and I drag Michael out. Right on cue he bursts into tears and runs off to his room. Also right on cue his father jumps up from the table, grabs Michael's plate, and trails after him with his meal. I'd rather he just left it and let it go cold to teach Michael a lesson.

Night after night, Michael gets to eat in his bedroom while watching his TV. This leaves the rest of us to tough it out at the dinner table with the older two complaining that they'd love to eat in their rooms with the TV on as well. I'm so frustrated with Michael's dinner time behaviour and his father's response to it.

Driven by fear
Our nine year old, Sofia, has always been a fussy eater. Only cucumber sliced thinly, never diced, and no other vegetables. When it comes to meat, it's only chicken schnitzel smothered with tomato sauce.

We often hear, "I'd rather starve than eat this." Instantly my partner hits and roof and pulls out the photos of our African sponsor children. He launches into his usual lecture about food, nutrition and privilege. I see his point, and I know she needs to hear it, but it all falls on deaf ears. She lives in her world and whatever he says, she can't apply it to her life.

One night she screamed at us, "You go on and on about food, food and food - do you want to turn me into an anorexic?" This sent a chill down my spine. Could our insistence that she eat cause an eating disorder? Should we give her what she wants to eat?

Now we're worried she'll develop an eating disorder.

Slow motion
Jacob, our seven year old, is a slow eater. He avoids putting food into his mouth to avoid chewing and avoid swallowing. Every mealtime I sit next to him and nag, bribe, entice and threaten, "Hurry up Jacob," "Jacob, eat," "Come on, less talking, more eating," "You'll be late for school," "You'll miss your TV show," "You'll make me late for work," "There's ice cream for boys who eat their dinner", "Jacob! We're tired of waiting for you to finish!"

I've checked in with our GP about his amazing indifference over food. She looked at me quizzically and asked if Jacob has any trouble getting through a bag of crisps or an ice-cream in a reasonable time. Of course he doesn't! Family mealtimes have become 'The Jacob Show' and we're tired of it!

Why adjust what's going on in your house at mealtimes?

If these stories sound familiar, we've got two great pieces of news for you! Firstly, 72% of respondents from our surveying tell us that at least one of their children's behaviour over food at mealtimes has a hefty impact on family harmony.

Secondly, it's never too late to make improvements because positive changes will advantage your child's wellbeing in the future. The frequency of family meals and well-adjusted adolescents is clearly linked. The research leads us to understand that emotionally well-adjusted teens eat meals with an adult in their family about 5 days a week, compared to 3 days for teens who show reduced emotional wellbeing. Studies indicate that these teens are less likely to get caught up in drug, substance and alcohol abuse, or become depressed (Bowden and Zeisz, 1997).

Eating dinner as a family provides valuable time for connecting, sharing and talking. Parents who influence how their kids think and help them cope with stresses, seize opportunities to talk with them and plant the right seeds in the right moments. Mealtimes can provide perfect opportunities to do just this and more!

achievement tests. This sole factor held greater importance than many other life factors (Cullen and Baranowski, 2000).

It's long been known that pre-schoolers from families that regularly eat together have better language skills than those in families who eat sporadically together. Researchers believe that extended, good-natured conversations provide young children with a chance to listen to language, build new vocabulary, contribute to discussions and think - this enhances linguistic development (Sanford, 1995).

Oprah Winfrey's famous 'Family Dinner Experiment'

In 1993, Oprah conducted her famous 'Family Dinner Experiment' (Oprah Winfrey Show, November 19, 1993). She challenged five families to eat dinner together each night for a month for at least a half an hour. All family members kept journals to record their feelings about the experience. At first, the families found this new experience really tough. It was a chore, and the promised half an hour commitment dragged! By the end of the month, however, each of the families wanted to continue eating dinner together (Parrott, 2011). The biggest surprise for parents was how much their children treasured the regular time with them at the table. Parents were also surprised by a common fact - that is, successfully sharing a meal together is a routine that requires repetition and refining - it just doesn't happen.

What about school performance?

A survey of 2000 high school students found those who ate dinner with their families four or more times a week scored noticeably better academically than those eating dinner with their families less frequently (Wildavsky, 1994).

Similarly, a University of Illinois study found that primary aged kids who spent more time eating meals with their families did better on school

The biggest surprise for parents was how much their children treasured the regular time with them at the table... successfully sharing a meal together is a routine that requires repetition and refining - it just doesn't happen.

Chapter 13:

Mealtime mayhem

Recipe rescue:

ideas to improve mealtime connections

This Recipe rescue is for families who see value in the ritual of regularly eating together and want to make it work. It is for parents who realise that 'breaking bread' together is an engaging way to build strong relationships because it gives everyone a chance to face each other, connect and spend time together.

First, think about what you really want? Our expectation about our children's eating behaviour is typically a high priority. Some of us adopt the same strategies our parents used because they're familiar and may have worked on us. However, many of us remember sitting in front of cold brussels sprouts or pumpkin until what felt like midnight, or worse still, being force fed by an angry parent. Most make a silent vow never to put their kids through that same suffering.

So what's the right way to jump? What sort of dinnertime behaviour are you getting at the moment and what's triggering it? Is the tricky eating behaviour being triggered by food sensitivities, or by an urge to grab power at the dinner table? How are you dealing with it? Are you loud, reactive and forceful? Are you matter-of-fact, nonchalant and disarming? Is your approach working? Have you set goals and are you working with an improvement plan?

Here are a few more questions to help you sort your thinking

If you had a magic wand and waved it, what would you want mealtimes to look like?
Make a list that captures your perfect 'vision'
What is it about this 'vision' that's important to you?
do you imagine everyone at the table together?
is everyone engaged in pleasant conversation?
is everyone enjoying the meal?
are there compliments being given about the meal?
are there happy faces and lovely warm exchanges?

How much of this is real and how much is from an old-fashioned dream world you cling to?
What's frustrating you?
Is it all going wrong, or is there a particular child who's pressing your buttons?
Do you feel as though your responses are being dictated by the kids?
When you're at work do you let others press your buttons this easily?
Why the difference?

What else is happening to jeopardise your 'grand vision'?
Are your children caught up in afternoon or evening sports?
Do you or your partner work late?
Is there too much pressure to get dinner ready, have dinner, do the kids homework, get them washed and get them to bed? Is this the problem?
If you asked others in the family about their vision of 'perfect' mealtimes together, what would they say?
How close would this be to your vision?
Do the kids, or your partner, actually have a vision?

What is it that you really want from mealtimes, from your partner and from your kids?

What you can do

You can make dinnertime an invitation for each child to join the family and share the meal - that's all it is, an invitation.

You can switch your thinking to dinnertime being an invitation for the kids to meet, share thoughts and eat. This instantly takes the pressure off of you when one of them chooses not eat what's on offer.

You can, treat it as a choice they've made when one of your children chooses not to eat, complains about the food or eats very little. And of course, all choices carry consequences. In this situation a perfectly natural consequence is that once dinner is finished there is no more food, and this child will go to bed a tad hungry. You might pop their dinner in the fridge for tomorrow. This won't make you a neglectful parent.

You can, by following this simple model, place your kids in charge of whether they eat or not - they are no longer dictating your emotional responses.

You can let these consequences play out without going on and on, without enticements, and without saying, "I told you so" and giving it too much attention.

You can put the kids in charge of their consequences. When kids know that a meal will be available for a set time and then be removed, eaten or not, they can start to exercise choice about when they begin to eat, how fast or slow they eat, or what order they eat the foods in. This is great for them - your certainty puts them in charge.

You can decide to recognise fussy eating as a stage. It is real, and will go as quickly as it came as long as don't need to buy into it.

You can subscribe to a 'no-nag' policy. Do you think your nagging helps? Come on, be bold - who's the adult here? Change your behaviour and theirs will follow.

What you can't do

You can't make anyone eat. Your nagging, ranting, coaxing, bribing, threatening or smacking might result in a few more morsels being reluctantly swallowed, but that's all you're doing - your behaviour will not yield reasonable, sustainable or healthy longer term outcomes! It will guarantee that you see more tricky and oppositional mealtime behaviours from the kids.

Hunger - it's a basic drive!

Never forget the universal strength of hunger. When the body tells us it needs food and fluid, we must eat and drink. However, a number of parents with kids who've developed reactive eating behaviours fervently argue this point! They maintain that their kids are 'a special case'.

So what's happening in these families? Plainly put - the kids have convinced their parents they'll starve rather than eating the reasonable selection of foods that have been served up to them. The thinking of these parents has become as gooey as 'mushy peas'. These kids have learnt that they have a devoted audience, and boy do they play it accordingly. They've learnt that the emotional tone of the family hangs on their every mouthful, that they are in charge and have a special power at mealtimes. Their parents have forgotten that hunger is a powerful basic drive!

Grazing, overeating and hunger

There's been a lot said about the health benefits of grazing throughout the day compared to having three meals. If grazing works in your home, then more power to you! Nonetheless, it is essential to monitor how much our kids are eating between lunch and dinner because eating can be great way to ease boredom. It might be that the snack here and there is adding up to a child who has had plenty of food before they get to dinner! Constant snacking throughout the day can leave kids less hungry and disinclined to eat dinner, let alone try new foods.

To be safe, try to stick to a consistent meal and snack ratio - allow at least two hours between your children's after-school snack and dinner. Work on delivering two or three snacks a day, and limit them to about 150 calories or 600 kilojoules a piece - promote fruit and avoid high GI, high fat or high sugar hits. This way, your kids will be more likely to want to eat at mealtimes because they actually 'feel' hungry.

Another trick that works a treat in our households is replying to, "Can I have something to eat" with "Have a glass of water and come back and see me in ten minutes if you're still hungry. Often a thirsty body switches on a hungry feeling.

Who's really hung up on power?

Do you ever cringe when you replay what you've said to the kids about food at mealtimes?

"You will not leave the table until you eat everything."

"That's right. I've spent the last half an hour slaving in the kitchen, but do you care?"

"Do you ever think how hard I work to put good food on the table for you?"

"Stop it! And stop it now! This is good food and you'll eat every bit."

"I don't care how long you have to sit at the table!"

"While you sit there think - 'what are the poor kids eating tonight? Do they have anything?'"

"If you screw your nose up at that meal I'll sell your iPod touch on eBay"

"I'm sick and tired of your nonsense."

"What's wrong with you? Most kids would be grateful for this."

What you're serving up to your kids is more than food. You're serving up a grab at power, and to seize it back, you have served up a distasteful selection of thoughts and feelings. You've encouraged your child not to care, to raise the stakes and desperately create a way to avoid letting a single crumb get past their lips, even though they know you'll go ballistic.

Make no mistake, you are caught in power grabbing behaviour by continually hovering over your child, monitoring their every bite and saying - "hurry up,""get on with it,""what's wrong with you?""Eat your vegetables before you…,""be a good boy and eat up,""come on, do it!" It communicates to your child that you are the boss of what they eat, when they eat and how much they eat. There is little choice for them. It plays right into the hands of the dinner-time attention seekers and if they have an oppositional side to their personality, then… it's game on!

This is the moment to think how a skillful manager performs at work. They'll set realistic deadlines, make expectations clear, be optimistic and will then quietly back off to avoid micromanaging. They allow staff to make decisions and run with it. You see, they know micromanagement destroys motivation and loyalty. Just like the manager's staff, kids need to hear genuinely encouraging words from you - that's all! Yes, if you're in the habit of controlling through nagging and browbeating, becoming a skilful manager will require much more self-discipline from you than the one you've been using so far.

Be careful to shine your spotlight in the right direction

'Attention needy children' see mealtimes as an opportunity to grab the spotlight and fire up their parent's anxious participation. So, here's a timely reminder. When we give attention to a child, we shine a spotlight on them, and on that very behaviour. By giving attention to that behaviour we are saying, loudly and clearly, that the behaviour gets our attention. We reinforce and strengthen the behaviour so it will continue! So, where are you shining your spotlight at mealtimes? Do you shine it on cooperative, or on annoying behaviours? Is your effort worth a rethink?

Be careful to catch the behaviours you value and want to see more of. Be sure to use, not overplay, words of encouragement;

"Thanks for saying thanks!"

"Those manners are sparkling today."

"Boy, that food is in trouble!"

"It's just a pleasure to watch you eat like that."

"You sit up to the table like an expert."

"It's wonderful to have dinner with you."

"You're eating beautifully."

Man, can somebody rescue that chicken?"

Shift from your usual food focus to dinnertime conversation; go around of the table and invite each person to share a funny thing that happened during the day! Plan a weekend outing, discuss and decide on a family issue - healthy family conversation moves the spotlight away from uncooperative eating. This may help your child, but see it as support for yourself. Expect that once you shift your spotlight from the 'usual' annoying behaviours, your child is likely to put in a special effort to be more irritating for a while. Their eating may get slower, they might conjure up a cough, gag, a spill or a dropped utensil. This is the time that your resolve and composure counts the most. Ignore it and keep the conversation going. When one of the other kids points out that their sibling is not eating, just say "thanks" and continue on with the conversation. Go on, we challenge you to be that bold

Case Study; let the clock do the talking

Here's a winning plan. First comes Dad's reminder before dinner, "Kids, dinner will be served in ten minutes. See you at 6:15 at the table." He walks off stiffly after using his best English butler's voice! Next is a prompt as the kids start dinner; "Remember that dinner finishes at 6:45. That's when your plate will magically disappear!" He's made it clear what will happen and knows that focussing his attention on an uncooperative child will shift them into an oppositional gear and once that kicks in, kids not only say 'no', but relish the battle that ensues. This father knows how-to sidestep power struggles and he won't buy into how slowly any of the kids might choose to eat! When ten minutes are left he announces, "Main course closes in 10 minutes."

When dinner-time finishes he stands and transforms into butler mode saying, "It's been a pleasure sharing a meal with you all. The table will now be cleared and dessert will be served to those who've done their best to eat dinner". Then he whisks the plates away despite the possibility of tears or tantrums. He doesn't lecture the unhappy child about their poor choice. Instead, he responds empathically, "I know you're disappointed, but you can make a different choice tomorrow night". Then he moves away and prepares dessert for those who made an effort.

When his disappointed child begins to hurl emotional grenades like, "you don't love me," "you're mean," "you hate me," "I hate you, "...he's ready to either tactically ignore, or say "I'm sorry you feel that way" or "I love you way too much to argue."

Plan meals ahead

By planning ahead we're talking about anything that supports you to be in best emotional state when the kids' tricky mealtime behaviour starts. Here are several tried and tested ideas;

prepare the meal, or a good part of it, earlier on when the kids aren't around

- ☑ Get organised and create a weekly menu
- ☑ Encourage the kids to contribute to the menu so each of them feel as though their tastes are being met
- ☑ Display the weekly menu on a whiteboard/ poster so that everyone in the family is aware of what's upcoming
- ☑ Remember, problems with food choices always start in the supermarket and play out at home - think carefully about what you want in your pantry. Think; 'is what I've got sitting in the pantry helpful, nutritious or distracting or detrimental?'

These ideas won't necessarily stop the kids from testing you at mealtimes, but as their pressure mounts you'll be in the best position to remain calm and committed to your new plan.

Have some fun - film 'practice nights'

Set up two 'practice nights' for the family to rehearse how-to eat a meal together. Seems crazy? Not at all - just watch what happens. You may wish to grab your iPad, or similar, and make a movie to show others how it should work at the dinner table!

Night One:

Discuss the idea of a perfect mealtime and ask the kids to come up with a list of behaviours that would occur. Decide on the top five most important behaviours. These might include;

- staying at the table
- sitting sensibly on your seat
- chewing with mouth closed
- elbows off the table
- eating without being distracted
- eating quietly
- keeping the food on your plate
- making a positive comment about the food
- having positive conversation
- encouraging others to speak and share their opinions
- speaking kindly and asking thoughtful questions
- using a knife and fork
- asking politely for something to be passed to you

Night Two:

It's time to put this into action. Make this first video just 2 minutes long. To begin, review the top five behaviours that must be seen. Start by getting one of the kids to say, "action!" At the end of filming, review the video together. Ask the kids to evaluate the family's performance as a score out of five (holding up fingers). If the shared opinion is that it's pretty good suggest sending it to a grandparent, relative or close family friend. Make sure you forewarn them to receive it, and ask them to dare the family to make a longer version! Resist the urge to do this too often. It's best to leave the kids wanting more. When you do it next time, make sure that you're doing it to meet a challenge from that loving grandparent, relative or close family friend. The reward for a perfect video might me a meal in a 'fancy restaurant' where the family can use these skills in public.

Serve small

Many kids are overwhelmed by the sheer volume of food on their plate and a few parents are over the top about kids having to clean their plates up. A sensible approach is to serve half portions and let the kids know they can come back for seconds! Small serves look achievable. Imagine the sense of accomplishment for a child who is not used to getting close to finishing. The thrill is enormous; for them and you!

Encourage the kids to eat until they are comfortably full, and, even if it's against your better judgement, believe them when they say they're full. It is reasonable to consistently encourage your kids to try a little of the foods they prefer less each time. Over time, as the food becomes more familiar to them, and their palate matures, they are likely to be more open to new and different, tastes and textures. But, don't get side tracked; there are habits more important than "Eat all your vegetables" or "Clean that plate up" that we're focussed on.

Use 'Grandma's Rule'

Grandma's rule, also coined the Premack Principle by Professor David Premack in 1965, suggests that individuals will do a less desirable activity to get to a more desirable activity. In terms of mealtimes, 'Grandma's Rule' traditionally went like this; "Eat some of your broccoli and then you can have ice cream for dessert." If a child then decides not to try the broccoli, there's no dessert - and that's the end of the story! Generally speaking we subscribe to 'Grandma's Rule', but we suggest being cautious. Be careful not to position dessert as an ultimate prize, and something to be valued above other foods. Perhaps this is the time to introduce two new phrases to your children; "nutritious food - food that looks after your body" and "junk food - high fat and sugar mixtures that trick the brain to feel good".

We prefer; "I'll only get ice-cream for those who've tried their best." Notice the language? You're stating what you will do, not telling the kids what they must do. When serving desert to the others, never condemn the child who's missing out. It's okay to be empathic, even give them a cuddle and say, "we all make choices we feel sad about sometimes. You'll do better tomorrow night!" Snacks are not available later on for this child, but you knew that anyway, didn't you?

Above all, model good eating behaviours yourself.

What about breakfast?

Here's a solution one of our clients use when their kids decide not to eat their cereal at breakfast. Without a comment or undertone of disappointment, they secretly pour their child's cereal into an air-tight plastic container and pop it into the lunch box with a spoon. It takes the place of the treat they would have otherwise put in. Their child may not eat the cereal, but as you've gathered, that's not the point! Oh, if this is too uncompromising for you then make it known, and stick to it, that treats only go into the lunch boxes of those who've given eating breakfast a good effort.

No, not a RED CARD!

Martina found that her children - Joe 9 years, Mai 7 years and Oskar 5 years - had become so used to her telling them to hurry up over breakfast that they no longer heard her. However, she was resourceful and quickly hit on an imaginative solution. To begin, she made 3 sets of cards. There were 3 cards; white, yellow and bright red in each set, and each set had one of her children's names on it.

As Martina busied herself organising the kids, preparing breakfast for them and buzzing about the house she kept the 3 sets of cards on the kitchen counter. As soon as she noticed one of them up to no good, whining or going too slow on eating breakfast she'd deliver them a white card with their name on it.

No words slipped from Martina's lips. She'd smile, but the message was very clear to the kids - 'You know what to do. I expect you to do it. Now get a wriggle on!'

The next critical moment was when the clock reached 7.50am. Everyone knew that their plates, bowls and cups had to be taken to the kitchen sink, and heaven help anyone who hadn't eaten a reasonable amount of breakfast. If that was the case, and one of the kids was already holding a white card, then they'd receive a yellow card. Once again, Martina wouldn't say a word because the kids understood its meaning - "You know what's expected and you've ignored what you need to do. You are now sailing very close to the edge."

The final step was receiving a RED CARD! It meant there would be a consequence with some bite to it. Her children respected Martina's devilish sense of humour and the innovative consequences she came up with. Martina's ingenious mind worked overtime creating niggling, but highly appropriate consequences for those occasionally red carded! Endless consequences ranged from the loss of a privilege, dropping her children late to sport, to friends or to parties, to picking them up early from play overs, missing out on something, early to bed, time alone, writing an apology or taking on additional chores. Martina's children are now young adults and they speak ever so fondly of her behaviour management style throughout their childhood.

One way to entice positive behaviours is to set up a 'breakfast incentive scheme' where a breakfast eaten on time, earns big points! Where a breakfast not finished up, but given a reasonable effort, delivers a few points. It's always best to negotiate the points required for the incentive or reward in advance. Younger children rely on schemes that deliver incentives quickly as they generally struggle with delaying gratification.

My Notes:

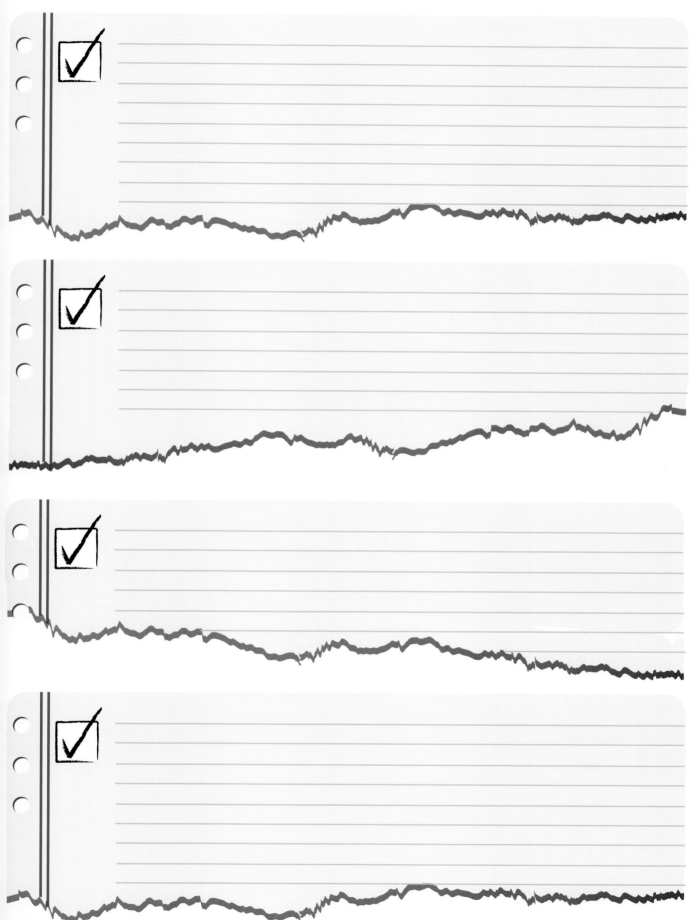

Case Study: 'No thanks'

"Andrew, my son had his birthday party last week and invited four friends from school. By the time the party was finished, I felt agitated. Nothing had gone wrong. I just didn't feel any warmth or connection with the boys. When they were collected by their parents I struggled to say it was a pleasure having them - something I'd normally say with openness to the parents of visiting children. It left me feeling disinclined to have any of them back over for a play.

A couple of days later my feelings about the boys crystallized. None of them said "thank you" for anything at any time. I replayed a moment where Thomas, one of the guests, looked straight at me and said, "I'm thirsty". This was the thing; none of the boys had shown manners during their visit - no 'please', no 'thankyou' and not one of them had been taught how to be gracious to the adult hosting the party.

I'm disappointed for the boys because they've missed out on being taught how to use manners. Their parents have put them at a real social disadvantage. I'm sure they're likely to make the same impression on their teachers, with other parents, with sports coaches, with scout leaders and eventually with their employers if someone doesn't teach them how courtesy works and why it works."

Case Study: First impressions count

"It was the second week of the new school year and Julianne's mum swept into my classroom as I was organising my class. I couldn't help but notice how attractive she was. That was before she opened her mouth!

"My husband and I want to meet about Julianne's progress" she said, expressionless.

Oh my goodness! Where was the "hello, how are you?" or, "Sorry to interrupt" or, "Hi, I'm Adrienne, Julianne's mum".

Before I could gather myself, she pulled her phone from her bag and clicked through her calendar.

"We're both free next Wednesday. I know you do staff meetings on Tuesdays, so I'm guessing Wednesday won't be a problem?"

I could feel my heart skip a beat and my blood pressure rising. "Sorry, I know you are Julianne's mum, what was your name?" I said.

"Adrienne," she replied, remaining aloof, without a smile and without eye contact.

I breathed out slowly, fighting every impulse to tell her that she'd get a meeting when she learned some manners and stopped assuming she and her husband were the only busy people in the picture. "Adrienne, I can't do next Wednesday as I have a curriculum meeting. I'll email you ..." She cut me off - shut me down!

"Peter and I are concerned that you are not challenging Julianne," she spat at me.

Now I was simmering. "There will be a meeting when I can find time

for one. I'll email you this evening with some times," I said clipped, but politely. "I have to get the children off to Japanese now." With that I turned and moved away.

You know, if she had of approached me showing a little care for me and for what I was doing, I would have met with her while the class was at Japanese. Perhaps it's unprofessional, but as she backed me into a corner I decided to make her wait for her meeting. I can see now why Julianne struggles with some of the staff and has built an abrasive reputation.

Maybe the apple hasn't fallen far from the tree!"

This is a chapter about manners

Watch a group of adults discuss manners. It's a moral, value-laden minefield and will soon divide the group. Whatever your opinion on manners, the fact is that over the centuries manners have long marked a difference between class and caste, they open or close social doors and determine who profits from available opportunities. Manners are an outward display of what's valued and because of this they are often the key to establishing rapport because 'people like people like them'. As we teach our kids manners we give them a better chance of being viewed favourably by others. In so doing, we set them up for a smoother ride through life, and it's as simple as that!

Manners:

a set of considerate behaviours that make us appealing to others.

Make no mistake, the way your kids present themselves to you, to friends, other parents, child care professionals, school staff, sports coaches, instructors, tutors, health care professionals and even employers will influence how their lives turn out. Manners will influence how much care and interest they receive from adults.

A father with a permissive attitude is likely to say, "It shouldn't matter whether the coach thinks my son is a nice kid or not, he should treat him the same as the other boys in the team".

We say - the coach is only human and despite his best multiple efforts, he's struggled to engage positively with this ill-mannered child. As he's a thoughtful person he's simply chosen to emotionally withdraw. What if the coach wasn't such a good person, was less tolerant and took offence to this boy's rudeness? Might he feel an urge to make life tough or teach this boy a lesson?

A mum also with a permissive parenting style states, "I've always taught Johnny to respect adults who show him respect first. Kids shouldn't have to automatically respect authority. That's an out-dated idea".

We say - mum's ideas just aren't right! Her son's time at school has been characterised by rocky relationships with teachers who consistently describe him as surly. Mum's created an obvious social shortcoming for her son. Johnny's problem is that others just don't like him, and because of this, their 'mirror neurones' reflect Johnny's negative attitude right back at him. Oh yes, there's a set of neurones in our brains that ensure reciprocal social exchange. Notice how a smile from a stranger will trigger your own smile, or a scowl from another is likely set off feelings of distain? It's all in our hard-wiring!

Chapter 14:
Manners

likable kids, likable parents

In this 'Recipe rescue' we're tackling the contentious subject of manners. Will you agree with all we have to say? Probably not! Our intention is to spark your thinking and promote conversations about good manners, courtesy and civility. There's just so much at stake, we owe it to kids to be talking with them about manners. Here's a list of our essential 'friendly behaviours' or manners that will give kids the best chance of appearing friendly to others.

> *Manners – they give kids a fighting chance to be liked by others*

When asking for something, use "please." When receiving, say "thank you"

The best way to teach "please" and "thank you" is to use them yourself. If one of the kids asks for something and "please" is missing, avoid responding for a moment and gently prompt them by saying with a smile, "When I hear the magic word" or "When you use please I will…". When giving something to a child, hold it and wait for the "thank you" before handing it over.

When you want to speak to an adult and they are talking to someone else, wait (unless there's an emergency). Then say "excuse me"

Tactically ignore the child who interrupts, or turn briefly to them and say, "I'm talking at the moment. I know you want me. Just wait for a moment." If we stop our conversation and attend to an interrupting child, we send the message that interrupting is an accepted way to get someone's attention.

Sounding disagreeable

Some kids are permitted by parents to freely voice their negative thoughts. This bad habit convinces others they are inappropriate and rude, and are worth avoiding. "I don't like that" "That's not how you do it" "So, I can do that too" "I don't like it here" "Oh, you got the cheap one" "This tastes awful!" "I've got better things to do than this" Next time you hear such phrases from one of your children privately say, "Hey, when you don't like something or disagree with someone, keep it inside your brain because saying it makes you look unfriendly." Learning that we can think one thing and say another is an important milestone in kid's social maturation. As children learn the value of tact and how to look after other people's feelings, they discover that honesty isn't always the best policy.

Be complimentary

Most of us give away too few compliments, but the delightful response a compliment brings reminds us how valuable they are. Talk with your kids about what a compliment is, how to deliver them and how to receive them. Let them know that giving a well-placed compliment is reassuring to every relationship. Optimistic feedback is one sure way to positively influence the behaviour of others.

Brainstorm suitable compliments and rehearse the best way of doing it. Here are a few ideas to kick off with:

"You look nice today mum"
(with or without a kiss)
"I'm glad you're home dad"
(with or without a hug)
"Thanks for cooking dinner mum/dad. It's great!"
"Thanks for working so hard to earn money so we can have all the things we need"
"Thanks for helping me with my homework"
(with a smile)
"It's great to see you"
"I like being in your class"
"That was great fun. Thanks!"
"You are a great mum/dad"
"I'm glad you're my sister/brother"
"I love you. You're the best"
"I like the way you do that mum/dad"

Finally, be sure to compliment others when your children are about. Consistently set the standard for them to model their behaviours on.

When people ask you how you are, tell them! Next, ask them how they are!

"How are you?" almost always follows "Hello" in a friendly exchange. How kids handle this part of the conversation is important. Model how this is done through rehearsal; where you greet your kids as if you've not met them before, and start up a conversation. Kids always giggle when adults play games like this with them. Setting up simple scripts is powerful and gives kids something to draw on when having conversations with others.

When you've been at a friend's house, thank their parents for having you

When we show this kind of appreciation it increases the chance of being invited back! More to the point, the host expects to hear, "thank you for having me over". When forgotten, it makes a guest look like they don't care, didn't have a good time or have bad manners. How do we teach this? By insisting that our kids say it, and like many other pro-

social behaviours we'd like our kids to show, we've got to model it ourselves.

When making a phone call, introduce yourself to the parent answering the phone. Then ask if you can speak with your friend

A child's performance on the phone is their first opportunity to make a good impression with the parents of friends. Failing to introduce themselves and flying straight into "I want to talk to Teegan?" is a big mistake. Coach them to get their 'words and voice tone' just right because the person at the other end of the line can't see their face. When appropriate, let your kids listen to you on the phone and keep an ear out when they're using the phone too!

Never swear in front of adults

We all must learn to pay attention to who is within earshot when we're talking. When a child or teen drops a swearword within range of adults it is a big social mistake. The adult may not

look offended, but the child or teen has just sent a damaging message about themselves. Teach kids that the language to use around adults is exactly the same language they'd use around their grandparents.

It's also important to recognise that for some kids, using bad language may be socially necessary within some friendship groups, but even in the most colourful of teenage groups too much bad language can attract negative impressions from others. Finally, discuss online language. The stakes are very high online because once swearwords are in an email, blog, kik, twitter, Facebook or any other form of social media, there's no getting them back. Others have lasting evidence of their offensive language, and who knows whose hands this may fall into.

Quickly apologise, even if the mistake was accidental

Saying, "sorry" matters! "Sorry" can rescue and repair so many situations. Have fun with your children role-playing situations where "sorry" might be helpful. Try "sorry" with a smile, a frown, a touch, a wink, a handshake, a rub on someone's arm or a hug. Coach your kids to understand that "sorry" isn't always an admission of fault and it may not always be accepted by another. However, it's a powerful gesture to ease resentment and allow relationships to heal. As difficult as it may be, say, "sorry" to your kids when it's necessary. It is incredibly empowering for a child to have an adult make it right with them through a sincere apology. It shows that we all make mistakes and models humility.

Cover your mouth and turn away when you cough or sneeze, and don't sniff or pick your nose around others

If you forget to work on this one you place your kids' in peril. Snot and flying mucus is uninviting - people don't like the look, or the sound of it! So much so, that between kids it can become a source of ridicule and teasing. Likewise, being coughed or sneezed on is one

Smiling happens naturally; it doesn't take much effort and costs nothing. With so much to gain, be sure to model it and teach your kids how to deliver a classic Duchenne smile

of the more horrifying things that can happen to people in day-to-day social settings. Let your kids know this and how to courteously deal with it. As for nose picking; it's not on!

As you walk through a door, check to see if you can hold it open for someone close by

Here is a small act that makes a lasting impression. Can you remember the last time a young person held a door open for you? If you do, how did you feel about that child or teen? It's impressive stuff!

If you come across someone who needs help, ask if you can help them

The starting point here is for us to put our Good Samaritan behaviour on display so our kids can see how it's done. Show them how to ask someone if they'd like help and then lend a hand. Performing selfless acts for others instantly engages kids into an emotionally deeper world and draws out a more sympathetic view of life.

When anyone helps you, say "thanks"

Teach kids to present a grateful attitude. Even when something is supposedly their right, the friendly way is to be polite, and humble. The classic assessment of character is called 'the waiter principle.' It's said that a person's character can be summed up by observing how they treat a waiter in a restaurant. Do they say "please" and "thank you"? Do they look the waiter in the eye? Do they engage the waiter in brief, friendly conversation? Or do your kids have a sense of entitlement in that they keep their eyes fixed on the iPad, DS or PlayStation, and expect you to order?

If somebody is sad or shares bad news with you, show that you care

The ability to show compassion and being able to comfort another is a basic capacity that human beings expect from one another. Do you display empathic behaviours in front of your kids? Our children never stop watching and learning from us! Explicitly teach them how to convey empathy. There are two steps required to deliver empathy, they are;

1. Say something that shows you understand how the other person is feeling.
2. Say something to comfort the other person or to give them hope.

Smile when someone smiles at you

"When you're smilin', the whole world smiles with you." (Armstrong, 1958)

When you smile at someone you trigger a serious mind-body connection in the left frontal cortex, the area of your brain that registers happiness. As they smile back at you, the same happens for them. A smile causes changes within our bodies, it;

- boosts the immune system
- increases positive affect
- reduces stress
- lowers blood pressure
- enhances other people's perception of you

The research shows that smiling brings about a higher level of well-being, less negative emotions and increased sense of competence (Zhivotovskaya, 2008).

Smiling happens naturally; it doesn't take much effort and costs nothing. With so much to gain, be sure to model it and teach your kids how to deliver a classic Duchenne smile

(http://www.youtube.com/watch?v=y3_bk9jHXrI).

Your manners and your kids

We want to place the spotlight on you because your child's manners - the abundance or lack of them - have everything to do with you. Our kids depend on us to see mannerly behaviour modelled, and rely on us to insist on their use.

We have a question to ask you. How do you conduct yourself in your dealings with your child's school - with teachers, school leadership and other school staff?

We know what you're thinking! You're thinking, what's this got to do with teaching manners to kids?

We've spent years in and around schools as educators, supporting kids, parents, and teachers to work together. We've seen the incredible synergies come from strong and friendly relationships between staff and parents. We've also seen a lot of toxicity spawned by conflict. This of course sends teachers and parents into self-defence mode. Once the 'blame game' begins, the best interests of the child are in serious jeopardy. Kids are always the most vulnerable. The 'parent-school relationship' is intensely significant as it's where children witness their parents interacting with adults who are not inside their regular social circle, but who are very important. This is where your good manners - how you speak about teachers, how you speak to them and how you deal with differences and deadlocks - play a big part!

Here's your starting point; remember that teachers are a genuinely caring group of people. You would need to look far and wide to find a group of professionals who are more emotionally invested in their clientele. By the same token, parents obviously care deeply for their kids. The magic ingredient is to genuinely listen to one another and try to find ways to build trust. We do our kids a huge service in developing their manners when they are able to witness us at our finest during the tougher times!

Manners:

want to know what teachers need from you?

We decided to conduct some research of our own. We surveyed a hundred and five primary teachers and ninety secondary teachers well known to us from a range of different school settings. They candidly responded to the three questions below;

Question 1: What makes parents look friendly and easy to deal with?

- When parents offer to help
- When parents want to make themselves known to me
- When parents make an effort to get to know me
- When parents attend information meetings so they know what's happening
- When parents respond to newsletters and return consent/risk forms on time - so helpful!
- When parents trust that I have their child's best interests at heart
- When parents ask, "is now is a good time to talk", and if it isn't, be willing to make an appointment
- When parents make suggestions that are genuinely kind and well intentioned
- When parents share positive feedback and good news about their child's learning with me
- When parents say 'please' and 'thank you' in our interactions
- When parents support me when I've navigated a tricky situation with their child and had to apply a consequence
- When there's a problem and parents come directly to me I feel trusted

Chapter 14:

Manners

Question 2: What makes parents look unfriendly and makes you want to protect yourself?

- When parents come in angry and act rudely towards me
- When, through anger, parents embarrass me, themselves, their child, and everyone within earshot
- When the anger of parents make the kids in my care feel unsafe
- When a parent corners me in the morning and chooses not to notice other parents who want to speak with me as well
- When parents try to justify their child's poor behaviour and consistently rescue them
- When parents choose only to see their child's perspective and don't trust me to be fair
- When parents bitterly challenge our account of a situation and will not accept what we saw and what we know
- When parents criticise us to other parents in the car park, coffee shop, or worse, on social media
- When parents openly criticise other children and parents, and gossip about them nastily
- When parents complain directly to the principal, or the Minister without bringing the issue to me first
- When parents intimidate or hurt me, or others
- When parents ignore communication from the school
- When parents continuously pester, complain, nitpick and criticise

Question 3: What's a good way for a parent to talk with a teacher about their worries?

- If you want to email me with a concern, please write it when you are calm. Angry or emotional emails stress us out
- Once you have emailed me with your concern, give me some time to get my thoughts together
  I'll get back to you and if I don't, please politely remind me - like you, I have many things to deal with at once
- If you think I've made a mistake, tell me politely. Give me a chance to explain my reason for doing what I did, or to apologise if I got it wrong
- If you have a concern about a discipline issue, raise it privately with me so your child witnesses how-to resolve a disagreement, respectfully.

The result:

'top tips' to parents about how to work well with teachers - for your child's sake

- Attend all information sessions, student-led-conferences, parent-teacher conferences, curriculum evenings, functions such as art shows, sports day etc. - this shows interest and it helps build an informal relationship with the teacher and the other parents
- Attend excursions and incursions if you are invited, and if you can. This is a great way to get to know the teachers and other children
- Consider becoming a parent representative for the classroom or a member of the school executive if you have the time
- Continue to show interest in what's happening at school with your child
- From time to time check in with teachers (face to face or email) to share your child's accomplishments, to offer praise or to thank them
- If your child has difficulty with their behaviour, scholastically or with friendships, we'd like you to trust and work with us. This is our work - it's what we're trained for and enjoy
- Remember that kids, especially teens, are trying to meet expectations from a range of external sources. This means that occasionally some of their behaviour at school will be unexpected to you and me

Good manners; "the oil that lubricates society" (Rowe, 2010).

We couldn't agree more! Without 'a good manners base' you limit your own and your children's opportunities. The idea of appearing friendly and sociable to others absolutely influences how much care and interest others decide to pay you. Help your kids to learn this!

My Notes:

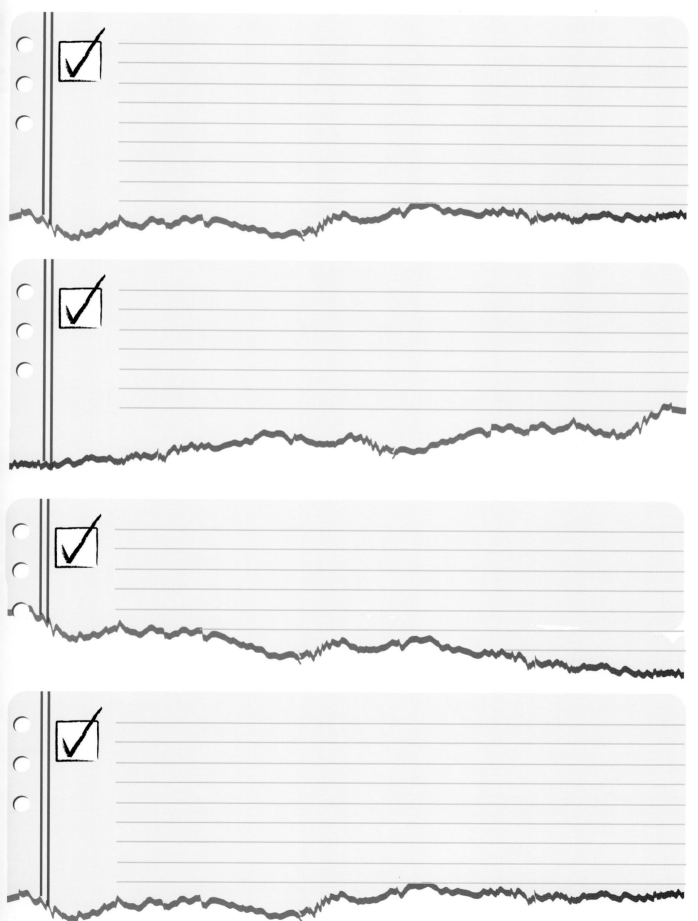

Recipe rescue:

critical ingredients to set kids up for success!

Thanks for reading, *Raising Beaut Kids: Recipes for parents on when to say 'yes' and how to say 'no'.*
We've had a great time writing it and learning as we've gone along.

We wrote it because Beaut Kids just don't happen! Even though kids don't come with instruction manuals, there's some study required! Kids need parents who've sorted out what matters most and are keen to develop a way of life that gives them the best chance. These are parents who have learnt to parent authoritatively - those who show good judgement, compassionate leadership and the capacity to develop predictable structures, boundaries and routines. These parents know when to say 'yes' and how to say 'no'.

While we've offered loads of easy, optimistic ideas from the 'Recipe rescues' to steer you in encouraging directions, our deeper purpose has been to ignite your thinking about how you choose to parent. When kids grow up feeling loved, secure and attached they are more likely to listen, be responsive, want to cooperate and

want to please. Yes, Raising Beaut Kids has as much to do with our relationship with them as it has to do with shaping their behaviour - the two go firmly hand in hand.

Regardless of life's circumstances, we believe being a mother or a father is the greatest contribution to humanity. What's more precious than shaping a young person to take on the world...?

Every parent navigates family life on their 'P-Plates'. So much of what we do with each of our children is for the very first time, and because it's a new experience, we're often wobbly about

it and feel there's a lot at stake. For most, life with kids has many tricky moments, yet despite the challenges, parenthood offers many joyful and satisfying experiences. For others, life hasn't worked out as planned or expected. Instead, it has become messy and complex with a mum or a dad feeling overwhelmed, or as though they're doing it alone. Regardless of life's circumstances, we believe being a mother or a father is the greatest contribution to humanity. What's more precious than shaping a young person to take on the world with compassion, independence, eagerness and wonderful emotional health?

Unfortunately, there's not a manual, silver bullet, universal rule or one magic recipe to guarantee that all kids will turn out well. Success isn't achieved with smoke and mirrors, magic or by enrolling your child in an expensive private school. What we do know is that our kids are deeply reliant on us to learn the healthiest patterns of thinking and living. To wrap up here's our ingredient list of critical ideas to set kids up for success;

All kids make mistakes and expect you to check their behaviour

This is a given. They rely on you to spot bad habits early and help replace them with behaviours that work better. If you must, describe your child's behaviour as 'tricky', do this in private or in your own head. Never label them as bad and never, ever refer to them as bad or naughty in front of others – as you do, you will create a self-fulfilling prophecy!

Support, rules, routines and boundaries

These make kids feel secure and safe. Invite kids to participate in developing a short list of rules around 'how our family works best'. Regularly meet together to discuss what's working and what's not. Keep talking and keep tweaking things. This is a twenty year project, but you know that don't you?

When you must, use negative consequences

Parents who are reluctant to use negative consequences create disoriented kids. If you worry about your child not liking you, remind yourself you are raising human beings, not participating in a popularity contest. Follow this rule of thumb; ask once, remind, and if your request is ignored, follow through with a negative consequence. Constant reminding, cajoling, pleading, moralising and martyr statements from parents create parent deaf kids who lose their bearings about what is and isn't fair, and their rights compared to the rights of others. Permissive parenting creates little monsters!

Deliver consequences that are natural and logical - never vengeful

Kids, just like us, learn best by gently facing their mistakes. Occasionally, when they're feeling overwhelmed your child might say, "I hate you!" Don't buy into this, they don't hate you. They just feel thwarted by you and are simply reacting to your correction. In this moment treat them with composure and respect, even though you may feel they don't deserve it.

Praise your kids often, genuinely and respectfully, when they deserve it

Praise is priceless. It gives kids the idea that we know they can meet expectations. It also lets them know that we're paying attention and are interested in what they're doing. Praise shows kids what we're looking for in their behaviour.

Avoid reprimanding your child in front of others

As tempting as it might be to show the world that you're a responsible parent, try to keep your reprimands private and your child's dignity intact. Embarrassed kids will only remember how embarrassed they felt - not what they did wrong and could improve on.

Help kids find their honesty

The quest for honesty is long and arduous. It's easily frightened out of kids who feel constantly criticised, disliked, unloved or backed into a corner.

Keep your perspective

When you go on and on about their misbehaviour it turns an error of judgement into virtual wickedness - be careful! Always think, "Am I facing a hiccup, a difficulty or a catastrophe? Will it matter tomorrow? Is it worth deflecting with humour, ignoring or dealing with?"

When you think you went too far and lost it, genuinely say "sorry"

This is important. Tell the kids it was an overreaction and you regret it - what great modelling! Please allow yourself to make a few mistakes because your mistakes allow the kids to feel warm towards you as they discover your vulnerability. It's a dangerous world when nobody admits their mistakes.

Avoid power struggles and extreme emotions

They will happen, but avoid them. The research tells us that what we've seen from the 1950's is a steady rise in rates of mental health problems, particularly for children and adolescents. Why? The link between too much stress in a young person's life for too long, and mental health problems, is now established. The consequence for kids who endure too much anxiety, tension, stress and uncertainty is for the rational, thinking, memory and immune system parts of their brain to become pruned. Their brain just doesn't set up as strongly as it should, and most of the action is switched to the emotional part of the brain. Parents who work hard at living happy, well-connected, balanced lives send a potent message about how to live life to their children. Do whatever it takes to keep your own emotional life in check. Your children's mental health depends on it!

Touch, hug and kiss your child affectionately and often

In the right moments kids need loads of quality attention, boundless approval and abundant affection from parents. This reassures them that they are loved and gives them the best chance to feel safe and confident. When you walk past one of your kids, touch, 'high 5' or kiss them! This is so important because we all need reminding that we are loved. This is perhaps never more important that in the moments after stern words or consequences. It shows kids that you can love them and disapprove of their poor behaviour at the same time.

Accept your child's personality

They need you to love and accept them - eccentricities, difficulties and all - so they can become attached to you and their siblings. So whether they are too shy or inquisitive, overly talkative, hyperactive or extremely impulsive, embrace them. Basic personality can be changed a little, but not a lot. Work at loving them for their differences. Their quirkiness may well prove to be their finest asset in the future, and, if their difference is a genuine part of their individuality, what messages are you sending to them as you constantly criticise their style?

Develop and maintain little routines

Working through the same series of steps each morning and evening, at the same time, sends a series of powerful time-place cues to the brain. These cues help all of us to switch-up in the morning as we prepare for the day and to switch-down in the evening as we prepare for sleep. Kids and teens rely on parents to have and apply a routine. Even fifteen year olds need consistent, explicit bed time cueing!

Kids need to make choices

Help your kids to build a sense that they can handle new or tricky situations. Encourage them to make choices even if it involves taking a sensible risk, and you know that they won't handle it as well as you would. When kids develop a sense of owning choices and decisions their competence grows.

Healthy, balanced relationships count for so much

Do you need reminding? Just watch the kids snap back, withdraw, stumble or become aggressive when we stay too grumpy and too removed from them for too long! Life with kids is always easier when we're able to keep a respectful and friendly air. Just try to listen to yourself sometimes or ask for some honest feedback from a loved one about how you conduct yourself in response to your kids. Life also improves when we deliberately build opportunities to connect with them - times to talk, listen, share, laugh and play. Arrange experiences with each of the kids you know will be enjoyable. The release of endorphins, our body's powerful feel good chemicals will strengthen your bond. Having a healthy, balanced relationship also means that when there's a hiccup, it doesn't have to skyrocket into a disaster.

Who parents best?

Regardless whether you're separated, divorced, share kids, run a blended family or joyfully live with a partner raising your own kids you don't need to parent identically. The parameters for healthy parenting are enormous, and to be the best parent you can you have to parent from your heart and personality while remaining firmly in the authoritative window (for a recap about the Social Control Window, see the Introduction). Trying to duplicate someone else's style isn't natural or sustainable. The bottom line - men and women think differently, approach things differently and as a result, must parent differently. Great mothers, broadly speaking, parent like wonderfully talented sheepdogs. They tend to nip at the heels of the kids herding them in the right directions, with the right messages so they reach their destination right on time and intact. Good fathers, on the other hand, are more like affectionate grizzly bears. Although most won't eat their offspring they're less likely to coax, cajole or charm a child into obedience. Once they ask a child to do something, they need action fast! When there's little or no action, they're prone to become grizzly, raise their voice and get demanding.

Parents can manage children differently and successfully. Kids cope extremely well with differences between parental attitudes and responses. They know mum does it her way and dad does it his way. What does not serve children well is continuing bickering between parents over who parents best. When we compensate for the supposed inadequacy we see in each other kids learn to play us off. Kids in these families quickly learn that there is so much tension between their parents that it's easy to get around them and get what they want. Do whatever it takes to avoid parental power struggles.

Fathers and sons

At long last the deep influence fathers have on their sons is recognised. Every contemporary fathering expert tells us that the quality of the father-son relationship is critical to the sort of young man that will emerge. Boys take a long time to grow and sons learn about being a man largely by watching their fathers.

"Above all, the father sets the model of how the son is to behave. And the son has to live with that. He can confirm to it, or rebel against it. Either way, a father puts his stamp on a son's life." (West, 1996, p. 82)

Boys are not born into the world knowing how to treat women. They watch how their father relates with their mother and through this, learns how to respect or disrespect women. A son also watches how his dad deals with conflict and differences, how he interacts with other males, how men relate with one another and how they deal with masculine issues. Too many dads step back, shrink, and become emotionally absent, convinced they cannot compete with the nurturance offered by their son's mother. This is tragic because a father's influence on his son is unmatched.

Finally;

Never underestimate the power of an emotionally connected and balanced family.

Remember, that there's no such thing as perfect adults, perfect kids or perfect families. They don't exist! We're all a work in progress. Even in the most limiting circumstance, parents who value the relationship they have with their children always make the greatest difference. So much of raising kids comes in the form of being a clever 'life-coach' who is prepared to gently, resolutely and intelligently chip away in the right moments. The best any of us can do is be real, loving, consistent, and continue to truthfully review whether what we are doing is advantaging our children's growth.

Are you ready to make a start?
If you are, begin by making one small optimistic change!

My Notes:

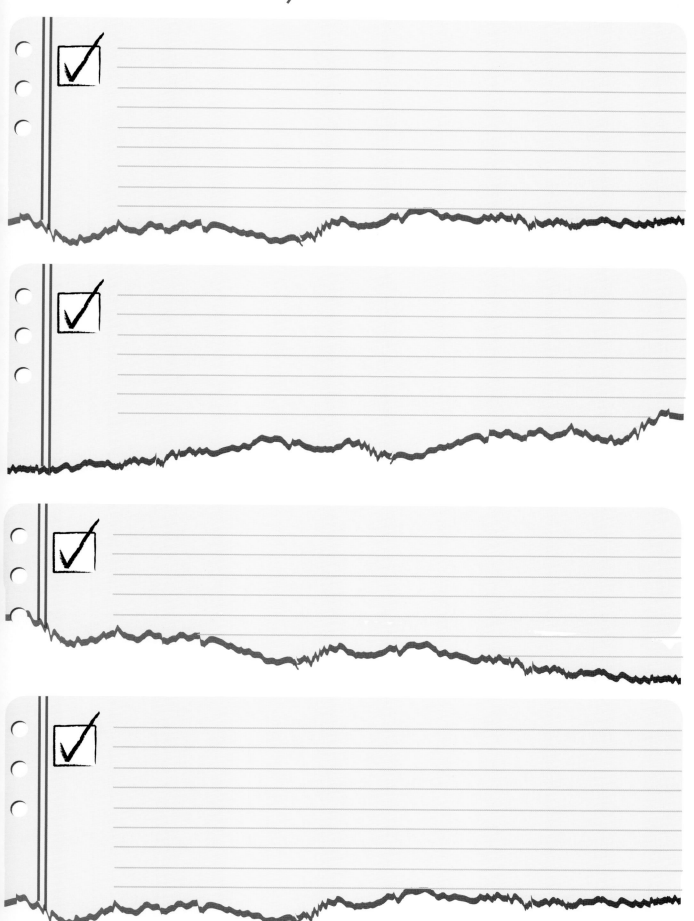

References

Introduction, Parenting in Windows

Kids Are Worth It!: Raising Resilient, Responsible, Compassionate Kids
Coloroso, B. (1994)
Canada: Somerville House Publishing.

Restorative Justice in Everyday Life: Beyond the Formal Ritual
In: Strang, H. and Braithwaite, J. (eds) Restorative Justice and Civil Society.
Wachtel, T. & McCold, P. (2001)
Cambridge: Cambridge University Press.

Chapter 1, Rules

Recipe rescue: building rules that work

The 7 Habits of Highly Effective People: Powerful Lessons in Personal Change
Covey, S. R. (2004)
New York: The Free Press

Chapter 4, Sibling Rivalry

Recipe rescue: steering sibling conflict in positive directions

Bidirectional Relations Between Authoritative Parenting and Adolescents' Prosocial Behaviors
Padilla-Walker, L, et al. (2012)
Journal of Research on Adolescence
Volume 22, Issue 3, pp. 400–408, September 2012

Getting Along: Sibling Fights
Oesterreich, L. (2004)
Iowa State University: University Extension
http://www.extension.iastate.edu/Publications/PM1651.pdf

Marital Conflict and Children's Functioning
Cummings, E. M. (1994)
Social Development, Volume 3, no 1, pp. 16-36

You can Do Nasty Things to Your Brothers and Sisters Without a Reason: Sibling's Backstage Behaviours
Punch, S. (2007)
Children and Society, Volume. 22, no.5 pp. 333-344

Chapter 8, "Get OFF that Computer, now!"

Recipe rescue: savvy ideas to balance the use of big and small screens

Effects of Violent Video Games on Aggressive Behavior, Aggressive Cognition, Aggressive Affect, Physiological Arousal, and Prosocial Behavior: A Meta-Analytic Review of the Scientific Literature.
Anderson C.A & Bushman B.J. (2001)
Psychological Science. Volume 12, Pages 353-359.

How long should kids watch screens?
Sigman A. (2012)
http://www.thesun.co.uk/sol/homepage/woman/parenting/4333139/Play-time-How-long-should-kids-watch-a-television-laptop-or-smartphone-screen.html

The Effects of Violent Video Game Habits on Adolescent Hostility, Aggressive Behaviors, and School Performance.
Gentile, D.A., Lynch, P.J., Ruh Linder, J., Walsh, D.A. (2004)
Journal of Adolescence, Volume 27, Issue 1, February 2004, Pages 5–22.

Chapter 12, Chores, Pocket Money and Saving

Recipe rescue: teaching kids to belong to the family by contributing

Resilient Children
Werner, E. E. (1984)
Young Children, November, 40. Pages 68-72.

The Richest Man in Babylon: Blueprint for Financial Success
Clason, G.S. (2007)
New York, USA: Bnpublishing Inc.

Think and Grow Rich: Your Key to Financial Wealth and Power
Hill, N. (2009)
Santa Barbara, USA: Success Co. Books

Chapter 13, Mealtime Mayhem

Recipe rescue: ideas to improve mealtime connections

Family Dinner Experiments.
Oprah Winfrey Show, November 19, 1993.

Influence of family dinner on food intake of 4th to 6th grade students.
Cullen K.W & Baranowski T. (2000)
Paper presented at The American Dietetic Association's Food and Nutrition Conference, October 2000.

Supper's on! Adolescent adjustment and frequency of family mealtimes.
Bowden B.S & Zeisz J.M. (1997)
Paper presented at 105th Annual Meeting of the American Psychological Association, Chicago, Illinois.

The Hour That Matters Most.
Parrott, L. (2011)
Illinois, USA: Tyndale House Publishers Inc.

Using 'rare' words at mealtime can enlarge children's vocabulary.
Sanford, C. (1995)
record.wustl.edu/archive/1995/09-28-95/4234.html.

What's behind success in school?
Wildavsky, R. (1994)
Reader's Digest. October 1994. Pages 49-55.

Chapter 14, Manners

Recipe rescue: likable kids, likable parents

Kids Are Worth It!: Raising Resilient, Responsible, Compassionate Kids
Coloroso, B. (1994)
Canada: Somerville House Publishing.

Manners Magic for Children
Rowe, P. (2010)
Australia: New Holland Publishers

Smile and Others Smile with You: Health Benefits, Emotional Contagion, and Mimicry
Emiliya Zhivotovskaya, September 27, 2008 – 2:32 am
http://positivepsychologynews.com/news/emiliya-zhivotovskaya/200809271036

When You're Smiling (The Whole World Smiles With You)
Written by Larry Shay, Mark Fisher, and Joe Goodwin Performed by Louis Armstrong, 1958

Wrapping Up

Critical ingredients to set kids up for success!

Fathers, sons and lovers
West, P. (1996)
Sydney: Finch Publishing.